VOLUME III

1922

THE LITERARY 1920s

"...and say my glory was I had such friends."—W. B. Yeats

KATHLEEN DIXON DONNELLY

"Such Friends": The Literary 1920s, Volume III—1922
©2022 by Kathleen Dixon Donnelly

Published by K. Donnelly Communications, Pittsburgh, PA, USA
Printed in the United States of America

ISBN (paperback): 978-1-7364831-4-5

ISBN (eBook): 978-1-7364831-5-2

Other books by Kathleen Dixon Donnelly, available on Amazon

"Such Friends": The Literary 1920s, Volume I—1920

"Such Friends": The Literary 1920s, Volume II—1921

Manager as Muse: Maxwell Perkins' Work with F. Scott Fitzgerald, Ernest Hemingway and Thomas Wolfe

Gypsy Teacher, a book of blogs chronicling the author's voyages sailing on Semester at Sea and relocating to the United Kingdom

Cover and interior designed by Lisa Thomson, LisaT2@comcast.net

Cover photo is James Joyce by Alex Ehrenzweig, 1915 cropped; and T. S. Eliot from Lord David Cecil and T. S. Eliot, 1923 cropped, by Lady Ottoline Morrell. Both images were obtained from Wikimedia Commons.

To Tony, Gerty and Bob

My "such friends"

"Think where man's glory most begins and ends,
and say my glory was I had such friends."

—The Municipal Gallery Revisited,
William Butler Yeats

PREFACE

To some, 1922 represents not just the most important year in "the literary 1920s," but the most important year in modernism.

Bookended by the publication of James Joyce's *Ulysses* in February, and T. S. Eliot's *The Waste Land* in the autumn, this year has been the subject of at least two excellent books: Bill Goldstein's *The World Broke in Two: Virginia Woolf, T. S. Eliot, D. H. Lawrence, E. M. Forster and the Year that Changed Literature*, and Kevin Jackson's *Constellation of Genius:1922: Modernism Year One.*

These two books have been fantastic resources for me, and I am privileged to own a signed copy of each. They are also two of the reasons why this volume of *"Such Friends": The Literary 1920s* is the thickest one in the series.

When I first heard about Jackson's book, I thought, "I can do that for every year!" But I decided to limit my efforts to the 1920s.

My original research, for my Ph. D. in Communications from Dublin City University, was about creative people in the early 20th century socializing in groups—salons. The four groups I focused on were:

- **William Butler Yeats** and the Irish Literary Renaissance,
- **Virginia Woolf** and the Bloomsbury Group,
- **Gertrude Stein** and the Americans in Paris, and
- **Dorothy Parker** and the Algonquin Round Table.

Since then, in the blogs I've been posting at www.suchfriends.wordpress. com about what was happening 100 years ago, and in this book series, I've expanded my research to also include the other important writers who were "such friends." Joyce, Eliot, Forster and Lawrence of course; but also Katherine Mansfield, Edna St. Vincent Millay, and Ezra Pound, for example.

The title for all the work I have done about these creative people is "Such Friends," from **Yeats'** poetic line, "say my glory was I had such friends."

The list of the writers and artists I included in each group in my original research—four of the key salons in the English-speaking Western world—follows this preface, and their names appear in boldface throughout the book.

The burst of creativity that became modernism was brought about by men and women of extraordinary talent and ordinary pursuits. They ate, they drank, they neglected their families. They praised and berated each other privately and publicly; they bickered endlessly. They complained about money and few had day jobs. And they talked. And talked.

That part of their lives is what I have tried to chronicle in this series.

By 1922, in America **Dorothy Parker** and the Algonquin Round Table are drinking and partying their way through the decade. In France, Americans continue moving to Paris to take advantage of a great exchange rate and cheap booze, and to listen to words of wisdom about writing from an American who has already been there for decades, **Gertrude Stein**.

In England, **Virginia Woolf** and her Bloomsbury Group friends are cementing their careers as writers and painters. But in Ireland, a new country—the Irish Free State—is being born, in the midst of an ongoing Civil War. That doesn't stop poets like **W. B. Yeats** from writing, or the Abbey Theatre from presenting both new and old plays every week.

Volumes I and II of *"Such Friends": The Literary 1920s*, covering 1920 and 1921, are available on Amazon in both print and e-book formats, along with this book, Volume III—1922.

Seven more to go!

If you live on a Pittsburgh Regional Transit bus line, I am happy to meet up with you and sign your copy.

You can dip in and out of the vignettes in *"Such Friends": The Literary 1920s*, search to see if your birthday is included, look for mentions of your favorite writers and artists, or read it all straight through from January 1st to December 31st.

Let's see what makes 1922 so special...

Complete List of "Such Friends"

The Irish Literary Renaissance (1897-1906)

William Butler Yeats, poet, playwright
Lady Augusta Gregory, playwright
George Moore, novelist, playwright
AE (George Russell), artist, poet, playwright
Edward Martyn, playwright, philanthropist
John Millington Synge, playwright
Douglas Hyde, playwright, translator, politician

The Bloomsbury Group (1907-1915)

Virginia Woolf, novelist, essayist
Vanessa Bell, painter, illustrator
Lytton Strachey, essayist, biographer, critic
Duncan Grant, painter
Leonard Woolf, editor, critic, publisher, political writer
Clive Bell, art critic, essayist
Roger Fry, art critic, painter
John Maynard Keynes, economist, essayist

The Americans in Paris (1921-1930)

Gertrude Stein, novelist, essayist, librettist
Alice B. Toklas, cook, publisher, writer
Ernest Hemingway, short story writer, novelist
F. Scott Fitzgerald, novelist, short story writer
Robert McAlmon, poet, novelist, publisher
Virgil Thomson, music critic, composer
Sherwood Anderson, novelist, short story writer
Man Ray, photographer, painter

The Algonquin Round Table (1919-1928)

Dorothy Parker, essayist, short story writer, poet, critic
Robert Benchley, humorist, critic, actor
Alexander Woollcott, critic, broadcaster, actor
Marc Connelly, playwright, actor
Harold Ross, reporter, editor
George S Kaufman, playwright, director
FPA (Franklin P. Adams), columnist, critic, broadcaster
Heywood Broun, columnist, sports writer, union organizer

ACKNOWLEDGEMENTS

The stories in *"Such Friends": The Literary 1920s* are compiled from a variety of sources, with details in the annotated resource lists in the back of this book.

For 1922, two authors, mentioned in the preface, deserve a special thanks: Bill Goldstein's *The World Broke in Two: Virginia Woolf, T. S. Eliot, D. H. Lawrence, E. M. Forster and the Year that Changed Literature*, and the late Kevin Jackson's *Constellation of Genius: 1922: Modernism Year One*. Having so much information about one year gathered together slowed me up a bit but was well worth the effort.

The beautiful design from Lisa Thomson and the production expertise of Loral and Seth Pepoon, owners of Selah Press Publishing, were so professional the last two times, we did it all again!

In putting together the list below of my "such friends" who have helped me in the writing of this volume, it struck me how many times I have called on some of you. I sincerely hope I haven't gone to the well too often, because I will need you for the next seven books too.

Once again, special thanks to my Irish-American husband and partner, Tony Dixon, and my work-from-home constant companions, Gerty Stein and Bob Benchley. And, once again, Liz and Kevin Tafel-Hurley have always come through—this time by leaving town so I could have writing weekends while cat/dog/housesitting for them.

For specific postings I am also indebted again for legal facts to Linda Tashbook; for sorting out Irish politics and history to Neil C. Weatherall, author of *The Passion of the Playboy Riots*; and for interpreting European history to Dr. Marie Hooper.

Rena McAllen and Peggy Dougherty of the Thoor Ballylee Society have been particularly helpful with details about **William Butler Yeats'** life in the west of Ireland.

I couldn't have done any of this without all of you.

Janie Ailes
Julian Asenjo
Alexandra Bassil
Jane E. Beckwith
Andrew Bucke
Michael Coyne
Clarence Curry
Joseph Davis
Barry Devine
Jim Doan
Peggy Dougherty
Patty Epps
Helen Fallon
Stephanie Farber
Gregory Grefenstette
Marie Hooper
David Hope
Mary Lou Irish
Cliff Johnson
Glenn Johnston
Nicola Jones
Maura Judges
Hedda Kopf
Carol Lytle
Alyce Marshall
Philomena Mason
Rena McAllen

Wylie McLallen
Emily Midorikawa
Jim Monteleone
Barbara Newsom
John Maxwell O'Brien
Robert O'Gara
Anton Perreau
Janet Purtell
Antonious Raghubansie
Chandrani Raghubansie
Debby Raymond
Mark Richardson
Scott Rossi
Nancy Ruffer
Richard Paul Skinner
Kathleen Spaltro
James Spates
Susan Snyder Sponar
Emma Claire Sweeney
Liz Tafel-Hurley
Linda Tashbook
David Trumbull
Eva Tumiel-Kozak
Neil Weatherall
Richard Webb
Mary Wiemann

❦ DECEMBER 31, 1921/ ❦
JANUARY 1, 1922
IRELAND, ENGLAND, FRANCE AND AMERICA

At the end of the second year of the 1920s...

In Ireland, at Dublin's Abbey Theatre, still directed by one of its founders, **Lady Augusta Gregory**, 69, the company is finishing up the run of a double bill including *A Pot of Broth* by one of its other founders, Irish poet **William Butler Yeats**, 56. The Abbey has been performing this little one act about gullible peasants since it was written over 15 years ago.

Throughout the country, violent atrocities are being committed by the Irish Republican Army and the British Black and Tans. In Dublin, in a huge leap forward for Irish independence, the

Newspaper headline, December 8

government of the Irish Free State is finally coming into being.

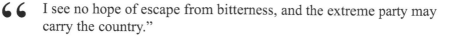

In England, near Oxford, **Yeats** is encouraged by the news of the signing of the Anglo-Irish Treaty, giving Ireland, including 26 of the island's 32 counties, Dominion status in the British Commonwealth. He writes to a friend that he expects the Irish parliament, the Dail, will ratify the treaty, but

❝ I see no hope of escape from bitterness, and the extreme party may carry the country."

With the establishment of the Irish Free State, **Yeats** and his wife Georgie, 29, are thinking of moving back to Dublin in the new year with their two children, Anne, two, and the recently christened Michael Butler Yeats, four months old.

In Sussex, **Virginia**, 39, and **Leonard Woolf**, 41, have come to their country home, Monk's House, for the holidays.

The Hogarth Press, the publishing company they have operated out of their home in the Richmond section of London for the past four years, is steadily growing. In total they published six titles this year, a 50% increase over last.

A book of woodcuts by a friend of theirs, **Roger Fry**, 55, that they brought out just a few months ago is going in to its third printing.

Their assistant, Ralph Partridge, 27, was at first helpful. Now he works in the basement, sleeps over during the week and has a bad habit of leaving the press and metal type dirty, which drives **Leonard** crazy. Partridge's profit-sharing deal has increased from last year but is only £125.

Before they came down here to ring in the new year, the **Woolfs** had a visit from their friend, one of their former best-selling writers, Katherine Mansfield, 33. They discussed excerpts from a new work, *Ulysses,* by Irish novelist James Joyce, 39, to be published in Paris early in the new

Katherine Mansfield

year. Mansfield agrees that it is disgusting, but she still found some scenes that she feels will one day be deemed important.

About three years ago, **Virginia** and **Leonard** were approached about publishing *Ulysses,* but they rejected it. They don't regret their decision.

In France, Paris has become home to over 6,000 Americans, enjoying being let out of the prison of Prohibition back home.

Writer **Gertrude Stein**, 47, who has lived here for almost 20 years, has been laid up recently after minor surgery. She is still writing, working on *Didn't Nelly & Lilly Love You,* which includes references to her birthplace, Allegheny, Pennsylvania, and that of her partner for the past 14 years, **Alice B. Toklas**, 44, San Francisco, California, and how the two of them met in Paris.

Because she recently visited the nearby studio of another American ex-pat, painter and photographer **Man Ray**, 31, who just moved here last summer, **Gertrude** works in to the piece "a description of Mr. **Man Ray**."

The author at Gertrude Stein's house in Allegheny, Pennsylvania

In America, New York free-lance writer **Dorothy Parker**, 28, is attending, as usual, the New Year's Eve party hosted by two of her friends from lunches at the Algonquin Hotel—*New York World* columnist **Heywood Broun**, 33, and his wife, journalist Ruth Hale, 34. Their party is an annual event, but bigger than ever this year because it is being held in their newly purchased brownstone at 333 West 85th Street.

Parker notes that they are directly across the street from one of the buildings that she lived in with her father.

Building across the street from the Brouns' brownstone

Dottie is here alone. Her friends don't expect her husband, stockbroker and war veteran Eddie Pond Parker III, 28, to be with her. They joke that she keeps him in a broom closet back home.

She's enjoying talking to one of her other lunch buddies, top *New York World* columnist **Franklin Pierce Adams** (always known as **FPA**), 40, who is professing his undying love for **Parker**. While sitting next to his wife and keeping an eye on a pretty young actress in a pink dress.

All the furniture except for some folding chairs has been removed to make room for the 200 guests and a huge vat of Orange Blossoms (equal parts gin and orange juice, with powdered sugar thrown in). No food or music. Just illegal booze.

As the turn of the new year approaches, the guests join the hosts in one of their favorite traditions. **Dottie** and the others each stand on a chair.

At the stroke of midnight they jump off, into the unknown of 1922.

Thanks to Neil Weatherall, author of the play, The Passion of the Playboy Riots, *for help in unravelling Irish history.*

❧ First week in January, 1922 ❧
Left Bank, Paris

When New York publisher Horace Liveright, 37, planned his month-long European trip, this is exactly the kind of evening he had hoped for.

His host and facilitator is American ex-pat poet Ezra Pound, 36, whom Liveright has never met. Through correspondence, Pound has been keeping Liveright abreast of all the latest publishers and writers working in Paris and London today, and this trip is Ezra's chance to introduce them to Horace.

Liveright had predicted correctly to his wife that this time in Paris with Ezra would be the "best of all" the trip.

Their companions for tonight are two of the ex-pat writers Liveright most wants to meet.

Ezra Pound *by Alvin Langdon*

American Thomas Stearns Eliot, 33, living in London but visiting Paris for two weeks, and Irishman James Joyce, 39, whose much talked about novel, *Ulysses*, declared obscene by the courts in the U. S., is nevertheless due to be published here early next month.

Liveright wants to sign up all three, and firmly believes in mixing contracts with cocktails. The rumor is that bootleggers visiting his Manhattan office often outnumber the writers. Eliot's favored tipple is gin, but the other three are not particularly selective.

Liveright would like to publish some of Pound's poetry, and he trusts Ezra's high opinion of Eliot's work.

Pound would like to see Eliot published more broadly, to get him enough income so he can leave his godawful bank clerk's job in London. In the two weeks they are here together in Paris, they are going to work intensively revising Eliot's untitled latest long poem. Pound tries pitching that one to Liveright, who is concerned it might not be long enough to be book-length.

Joyce would like to see *Ulysses* published in America but seems unimpressed with Liveright's offer of $1,000 upfront. Pound is aghast. Why wouldn't Joyce want that kind of money?

Pound is not aware that Liveright had offered to publish *Ulysses* once before. But he wanted to make changes; Joyce refuses to let anyone change even one word. For now, he will stick with the deal he has in Paris. American bookstore owner Sylvia Beach, 34, is bringing out *Ulysses* in a few weeks, word for word, the way Joyce wrote it.

❧ JANUARY 6, 1922 ❧
SCRIBNER'S, 153-157 FIFTH AVENUE, NEW YORK CITY, NEW YORK

Scribner's editor Maxwell Perkins, 37, is thinking about how to word this letter to one of his star authors, **F. Scott Fitzgerald**, 25, currently with his wife and newborn daughter in his hometown of St. Paul, Minnesota.

Scott's second novel, *The Beautiful and Damned*, is set to be published this spring. Max believes it will do at least as well as his first, *This Side of Paradise*, which was Scribner's best-seller of 1920.

Fitzgerald is also continually publishing short stories in widely read magazines such as *The Saturday Evening Post* and *Metropolitan*.

Maxwell Perkins

Perkins likes following a hit novel with a collection of stories by the same author, feeling that the sales of each will help both. This was true of *Paradise*.

For the follow up collection, **Fitzgerald** suggested a number of titles: *We Are Seven. A La Carte. Journeys and Journey's End. Bittersweet.* Or *Flappers and Philosophers*.

Perkins chose the last one, although Charles Scribner II, 67, president of the company, was aghast.

Perkins doesn't want to mess with success. Nevertheless, he wants to suggest to **Fitzgerald** that it might be time to take a different turn.

He knows **Scott** is in the beginning stages of thinking about his third novel. And Max is also concerned that his own four daughters might want to become flappers.

Perkins writes,

❝ We ought to...get away altogether from the flapper idea."

❧ JANUARY **10, 1922** ❧
28 RUE BOISSY D'ANGLAS, RIGHT BANK; AND
74 RUE DU CARDINAL LEMOINE, LEFT BANK, PARIS

French writer and artist Jean Cocteau, 32, has planned this terrific grand opening for the cabaret he is fronting, Le Boeuf sur La Toit (The Ox on the Roof), on the Right Bank. He and his business partners took the name from a ballet Cocteau had written a few years ago, to a catchy tune by French composer Darius Milhaud, 29.

Cocteau's own paintings are on the walls, along with others lent by Spanish artist Pablo Picasso, 40. However the centerpiece is the stunning painting behind the bar, *L'oeil Cacodylate*, by French painter Francis Picabia, about to turn 43.

Le Boeuf sur La Toit publicity card

It's almost midnight and the party is going strong. Picasso is here with his young Russian ballerina wife, Olga, 30. Welsh painter Nina Hamnett, 31, has arrived late.

Cocteau looks for his friend, French writer Raymond Radiguet, 19, and finds him at the bar chatting with Romanian sculptor Constantin Brancusi, 45. The two men aren't enjoying the party and, to Cocteau's dismay, grab Nina and take off to find a bouillabaisse.

To Hamnett's dismay, Radiguet and Brancusi abandon her at the Gare de Lyon to continue their search by hopping a train to Marseilles.

The Hemingways' apartment on rue Cardinal Lemoine

Over on the Left Bank, American ex-pats **Ernest Hemingway**, 22, and his wife of four months Hadley, 30, are settling in to their cramped, fourth-floor apartment above a *bal musette*, a bar with a dance floor presided over by the chain-smoking, accordion-playing owner.

The **Hemingways** arrived in Paris just a few weeks ago and have been staying at the nearby Hotel Jacob. An American friend found this apartment for them, with a mattress on the floor, no running water, and a toilet on each landing that they can smell when they climb the stairs.

The **Hemingways** are astounded by how cheap it is to live in Paris. In little neighborhood restaurants you can get dinner for two for 12 francs (about $1) and a bottle of wine for 60 centimes. Hadley's trust fund gives them $3,000 a year, and **Ernest** is working as the foreign correspondent for the *Toronto Daily Star*. They can afford to hire a maid to clean and cook them meals and can even afford to go on skiing vacations.

Today they are off to Chamby sur Montreux, Switzerland, for two weeks so **Ernest** can research a piece about the Swiss tourist trade for the *Star*.

If you now have Milhaud's catchy tune going through your head, you can hear the whole piece here. https://www.youtube.com/watch?v=9iqZ-lyUsNM

❧ JANUARY 13, 1922 ❧
BOMBAY, INDIA

Edward Morgan Forster, 43, can't wait to get on that ship tomorrow to begin his long journey home to England. Not because he is so looking forward to going back to living with his mother, Lily, 66, and his cat back in Weybridge, but because he can't wait to get out of here.

Last year Morgan accepted the bizarre job as personal assistant to his old friend Sir Tukoji Rao IV, 34, the Maharajah of Dewas state—always known as "HH"—in a spirit of adventure. Not only would he be away from Weybridge, but also he could finally finish his India novel, which he started before the Great War.

Well, Dewas, where he has been living for the past year, sure wasn't Weybridge. But he hasn't written anything except journals; he has published no new novels for a decade.

Every New Year's Eve—the day before his 1st January birthday—Morgan has made it a habit to write in his diary, summing up the previous year. This past New Year's he wrote,

> 66 India not yet a success, dare not look at my unfinished novel...how unsuitable were my wanderings at Dewas, where everyone laughed at my incompetence ...My desire for self-expression has slackened along every line...Slowness and apathy increase...I can't go on any more here."

In a letter home, Forster describes to his Mum the celebrations his friends arranged in Hyderabad for his birthday, filling his rooms with flowers.

> 66 It was roses all the way,"

he writes to her, always giving her the impression that he is happy here.

Morgan's plans for his journey home had included a visit to the Ajanta caves, which he'd always wanted to see. Then he fell and hurt his wrist and elbow so badly he couldn't even feed himself, let alone go hiking through caves. Another disappointment in India.

From Hyderabad to Bombay is 790 km, and now he is more than ready to set sail on the *RMS Kaisar-i-Hind* tomorrow. Rather than plan the shorter but more expensive trip back on land through Europe, he is going by sea to Port Said, Egypt, and then on to London. With the money he saves, Forster will spend a full month in Egypt. He explains to Lily that when he gets to Egypt he will be "nearer Mummy."

But his real incentive is that, in Port Said, he will spend the month with his lover Mohammed el Adl, 22. The last time they saw each other was for four stolen hours on a beach when Forster was on his way to India last spring. Now they will have much more time together.

❧ JANUARY 17, 1922 ❧
OAK PARK, ILLINOIS

Grace Hall Hemingway, 49, and her husband, Dr. Clarence Hemingway, 50, are eagerly reading the latest letters from one of their sons, **Ernest**, 22, currently living in Paris with his new wife, Hadley, 30, from St. Louis.

The Hemingways are at least glad that **Ernest** has decided what he wants to do with his life. Before the newlyweds left for Paris in December, he had a job, editing some company newsletter, but he was hanging out with his young friends a bit too much for Grace's taste.

Ernie and Hadley were eager to move to Europe—first they planned on Italy but decided on France. She has a trust fund to supplement his income as foreign correspondent for the *Toronto Star Weekly*.

The Hemingway home

Ernest writes to his parents that he and Hadley have moved out of the hotel they were staying in and now live in a fourth-floor walk-up apartment. Rent, food and drink are, thanks to a terrific exchange rate, really cheap. Dinner for both of them is 12 francs with a glass of wine! Grace hopes they don't spend too much of their money on that cheap wine.

❧❧❧

Elsewhere in Oak Park, another couple, the Whites, are welcoming their first child, Betty, born today.

❧ JANUARY 20, 1922 ❧
9 CLARENCE GATE GARDENS, MARYLEBONE, LONDON;
AND 70 BIS, RUE NOTRE DAME-DES-CHAMPS, PARIS

Tom Eliot, 33, part-time poet, full-time Lloyd's bank clerk, has been putting off writing this letter to Scofield Thayer, 32, publisher of the American literary magazine, *The Dial.*

Eliot didn't want to write more excuses why he can't submit his "London Letter" column again. Rather, Tom wants to suggest that he will continue the column, but, rather than reviewing specific books, he will write about life in England in general.

Eliot has been back in colder, more expensive London for just a few days, and he is missing Paris. He was supposed to return to his job at Lloyd's this week. But he's come down with (luckily!) a serious case of the influenza that's spreading around the country. And with his wife Vivien, 33, still in France, Eliot is working hard on finishing up his still untitled epic and would like to get it published as soon as possible. This forced isolation is a godsend.

Last fall, he'd been granted a three-month leave of absence from his job at Lloyd's. They agreed when, not only Viv, but also one of London's leading nerve specialists said Tom was having a breakdown. Tom spent part of his leave receiving treatment in Switzerland—which helped a bit—and the past two weeks in Paris working hard on the poem, collaborating (which he really enjoyed) with fellow American ex-pat poet Ezra Pound, 36, to cut it to the bone. Now Tom feels much more confident that this is his best work.

In his letter to Thayer, he assures the publisher that he will be able to send the finished poem along soon:

❝ It has been three times through the sieve by Pound as well as myself so should be in final form."

At 450 lines, in four sections, it can easily be spread across four issues of the magazine. Eliot also tells Thayer that the poem will not be published in England until he hears back from *The Dial*. Quickly, he hopes.

And, Eliot adds, he is curious as to "approximately what *The Dial* would offer."

Eliot doesn't mention that, at a particularly drunken dinner in Paris with Pound and Horace Liveright, 37, the American publisher expressed interest in having his firm, Boni and Liveright, bring out the poem in book form. If it is long enough.

꙳ ꙳

Meanwhile, back in Paris, Pound has been writing to Thayer, telling him to overlook Eliot's annoying characteristics and constant excuses. Pound really wants *The Dial* to publish this major poem, and he is trying to find other ways to get Eliot some income so he can leave that godawful desk job at the bank.

❧ BEFORE JANUARY 25, 1922 ❧
HOGARTH HOUSE, RICHMOND, LONDON

Virginia Woolf is about to turn 40. And she's not taking it well.

She is pleased to find out that her friend and fellow novelist, E. M. Forster, 43, is on his way back to England after spending almost a year in India. She writes to him,

> I was stricken with the influenza, and here I am, a fortnight later, still in bed, though privileged to take a stroll in the sun for half an hour—after lunch…
>
> Writing is still like heaving bricks over a wall;…I should like to growl to you about all this damned lying in bed and doing nothing, and getting up and writing half a page and going to bed again. I've wasted five whole years (I count) doing it; so you must call me 35—not 40—and expect rather less from me."

Leading up to the big day, in her diary she writes,

> [Life] consists of how many months? That's what I begin to say to myself, as I near my 40th birthday…
>
> The machinery for seeing friends is too primitive: 1 should be able to see them by telephone—ring up, & be in the same room… [But too many visitors leave me] in tatters…my mind vibrates uncomfortably…
>
> I have made up my mind that I'm not going to be popular, & so genuinely that I look upon disregard or abuse as part of my bargain… I'm to write what I like; & they're to say what they like. My only interest as a writer lies, I begin to see, in some queer individuality; not

in strength, or passion, or anything startling; but then I say to myself, is not 'some queer individuality' precisely the quality I respect?...

I feel time racing like a film at the Cinema. I try to stop it. I prod it with my pen. I try to pin it down."

Virginia Woolf's diary

❧ JANUARY 27, 1922 ❧

AMERICAN ART GALLERIES, AMERICAN ART ASSOCIATION, MIDTOWN MANHATTAN, NEW YORK CITY, NEW YORK

What a lovely day. Irish-American lawyer and art collector, John Quinn, 51, has some business at the American Art Galleries, where the Kelekian Collection is about to go on sale. He has decided to invite along Irish painter John Butler "JB" Yeats, 82, father of Quinn's friend, Irish poet **William Butler Yeats**, 56.

Since **Yeats'** dad has been living in New York for the past few years, Quinn has basically been taking care of him.

Quinn has arranged for a Packard touring car and driver and had his assistant (and mistress), Mrs. Jeanne Foster, 42, go on ahead to pick up JB. She has wrapped him up nice and warm against the bright chilly day, and they have met John at the gallery.

The three are having a great time looking at the paintings. Quinn is interested to see how the sale goes overall, because it will be an indication of the worth of his own similar—but much superior, in his view—collection.

Mr. Yeats and Mrs. Foster are both just enjoying being surrounded by such works of art. Corots! Courbets! Cezannes!

Quinn admires the self-portrait by Toulouse Lautrec. JB says that, the way that man looks, he should be guillotined. They make fun of a pastel by Degas. JB calls it "the washer woman exposed." Quinn asks their opinion of the Seurat, *La Poudreuse*. They both agree that it is lovely.

Quinn can tell that the old man is starting to tire, and his cough is getting more distressing. But he is definitely enjoying Jeanne's company.

Quinn bundles them both into the Packard to have a restful lunch, do some shopping, then end up back at JB's rooms. Quinn goes back into the galleries to determine how much to bid for *La Poudreuse* at the upcoming auction.

❧ JANUARY **30, 1922** ❧
VICTORIA PALACE HOTEL,
6 RUE BLAISE-DESGOFFE, PARIS

New Zealand-born writer Katherine Mansfield, 33, is concerned that she really can't afford to stay in this hotel that she has just checked in to.

Separated, once again, from her English husband, writer John Middleton Murry, 32, she is quite broke, even though her short stories are being published fairly regularly.

But she can't afford the treatments she has come to Paris for either, at 300 francs a session.

Mansfield heard about this Russian doctor, Ivan Manoukhin, 33, during the past few months when she was receiving treatments in Switzerland. She decided it would be worth a try to come here to Paris before returning to England.

Manoukhin uses low dose radiation of the spleen. She'll find out more tomorrow when she goes to his clinic. Nothing else has worked to cure the tuberculosis she has been fighting for the past four years.

✵ FEBRUARY 2, 1922 ✵
GARE DE LYON, PLACE LOUIS-ARMAND, PARIS

Standing on the platform at the Gare de Lyon, American ex-pat Sylvia Beach, 34, is waiting for the Paris-Dijon Express, due in at 7 am.

The first copies of the novel *Ulysses*, by Irish ex-pat James Joyce, 40 today, will arrive from Darantiere, the printer in Dijon. Sylvia's little Left Bank bookstore, Shakespeare and Company, has taken on the responsibility of publishing the controversial book when no one else would.

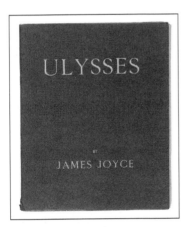

Ulysses *by James Joyce*

When Beach told Joyce that Darantiere guaranteed to mail the parcel on 1st February, Joyce was not pleased. He insisted that the package be put on the train so the conductor can hand deliver the two copies to Sylvia personally.

As the train approaches, Beach is working out the next steps in her head. She will get a taxi to Joyce's apartment at 9 rue de l'Universite to give him the 40th birthday present that he wants most, the first copy of *Ulysses*.

Then she will continue on to her shop, at 12 rue de l'Odeon, about 20 minutes away, to put the second copy on display in the window. Word has been circulating around the Left Bank that the book will soon be available, and those who subscribed in advance are eager to get their copies.

Tonight Joyce has planned a small party at one of his favorite restaurants, Ferraris, to celebrate his accomplishment, eight years in the making. He and his partner—and the mother of their two children—Nora Barnacle, 37, have invited just a few friends. One of Joyce's most loyal supporters and drinking buddies, American writer **Robert McAlmon**, 26, left town for the Riviera just yesterday. Didn't even leave behind a birthday present.

❧ FEBRUARY 3, 1922 ❧
9 RUE DE L'UNIVERSITE, PARIS; AND
31 NASSAU STREET, NEW YORK CITY, NEW YORK

Irish ex-pat writer James Joyce, 40, cables one of his main benefactors, Irish-American attorney, John Quinn, 51, at his Manhattan law office:

POSTAL TELEGRAPH   COMMERCIAL CABLES

TELEGRAM

The Postal Telegraph-Cable Company (Incorporated) transmits and delivers this message subject to the terms and conditions printed on the back of this blank.

| COUNTER NUMBER. | TIME FILED. | CHECK. |

Send the following message, without repeating, subject to the terms and conditions printed on the back hereof, which are hereby agreed to,

ULYSSES PUBLISHED. THANKS.

Quinn, meanwhile, cables to his friend, Irish playwright **William Butler Yeats**, 56:

🥀 FEBRUARY 5, 1922 🥀
PETITPAS, 317 WEST 29TH STREET,
NEW YORK CITY, NEW YORK

After the funeral, Irish-American lawyer John Quinn, 51, and his assistant (and mistress) Mrs. Jeanne Foster, 42, have come back here, to the Lower East Side boarding house where the Irish painter, John Butler ("JB") Yeats lived for most of the past 15 years that he has been in New York City.

Father of Quinn's good friend, Irish poet **William Butler Yeats**, 56, JB died two days ago, age 82, feisty and working right up until the end. His unfinished self-portrait, which he was painting on commission from Quinn, hangs here in his bedroom.

The old man had come to New York with his daughter for a holiday visit and just decided to stay, despite constant entreaties from his family to come home to Ireland. As he explained to them, a friend had told him that

John Butler Yeats' Self-portrait

❝ In Dublin it is hopeless insolvency. Here it is hopeful insolvency."

Quinn has kept an eye on him, and, as JB became more unwell in the past year, had taken care of him with help from Jeanne. **Willie Yeats** would sell his original manuscripts to Quinn but tell him to use the money to pay for his Dad's upkeep.

JB was quite active—going out for breakfasts, coming to Quinn's for Sunday lunch, staying up late talking to friends—up until a week or so ago. He had gone to a poetry reading out in Brooklyn, and, confused, took the wrong subway and ended up walking too long in the cold winter air. Since then his cough had worsened, and his health had generally gone downhill.

Now Quinn and Foster are surveying the room, filled with the life of this old artist. **Yeats** and his sisters will let them know if their dad is to be buried in Ireland in the spring, or laid to rest here sooner. Jeanne has suggested a spot in her family plot in the Adirondacks.

Jeanne Robert Foster *by J. B. Yeats*

In the meantime, they will have to go through the papers and the pictures to determine what to throw out and what to send back to Ireland. **Willie** wants his sisters' Cuala Press to bring out a volume of their father's correspondence.

On an easel in a corner of the room is another of his unfinished works, a drawing of Jeanne. JB's last words to her as she left him on Thursday night were,

❝ Remember you have promised me a sitting in the morning."

✠ FEBRUARY, 1922 ✠
82 MERRION SQUARE, DUBLIN; AND
4 BROAD STREET, OXFORD, ENGLAND

Georgie Hyde-Lees Yeats, 29, is proud of herself for buying the lease on this Georgian town house in Merrion Square, using her own family money.

The Anglo-Irish Treaty has been ratified by the Dail (although by a very small margin, 64 to 57) and they have elected Arthur Griffith, 49, president; British soldiers are being sent home from the barracks they have been living in throughout the War for Independence; and Michael Collins, 31, has been named chair of the new Irish Free State. Georgie and her husband, Irish poet and playwright **William Butler Yeats**, 56, have decided it is time to leave Oxford, where they have lived for the past few years, and move their two young children back home to Dublin.

Thanks to depressed housing prices in the city and Georgie's shrewdness in lining up tenants for the top floor of their new house, they will be able to afford the move.

✠✠✠

Back in Oxford, Georgie's husband, **Willie**, is impressed with his wife's real estate skills. He never thought he'd ever be able to afford to live in posh Merrion Square, birthplace of the Duke of Wellington and, in **Yeats'** mind, the Dublin equivalent of London's posh Berkeley Square.

Also, his father, the painter John Butler "JB" Yeats, died at the beginning of the month, aged 82, in New York City where he had been living for the past 15 years. **Willie** and Georgie had been supporting his Dad financially, and it's been a bit of stretch for them.

The letters JB wrote to his family in the weeks before his death are still arriving.

Oxford, Broad Street

❧ FEBRUARY 8, 1922 ❧
27 RUE DE FLEURUS, PARIS

The young newlyweds, about to knock on this door, are filled with nervous anticipation.

Toronto Star foreign correspondent and would-be novelist **Ernest Hemingway**, 22, and his new wife, Hadley, 30, moved to Paris in December. But they have waited until now to make use of one of the letters of introduction given to **Ernie** by his mentor, successful novelist **Sherwood Anderson**, 45, back home in Chicago.

When the couple told him they were planning to move to Europe—where **Ernest** had served in an ambulance corps during the Great War—**Sherwood**

27 rue de Fleurus

convinced them to choose Paris. They should join the other ex-patriates here, taking advantage of the great exchange rate. And he gave them letters of introduction to the creative people he had met here last summer, none more important than the woman who lives at this address, **Gertrude Stein**, just turned 48.

Stein is already legendary for the salons she and her brother Leo, almost two years older, had hosted here before the War, with the most cutting-edge painters of the time. **Gertrude** has said that she wants to do with words on the page what those artists are doing with paint on the canvas.

Sherwood is a huge fan of hers, so **Ernest** is eager to meet this woman and learn more about writing from her. But he is a bit intimidated too.

⁂

Gertrude is impressed with the young American writer she has just met. Very good-looking. **Stein's** partner, fellow American **Alice B. Toklas**, 44, had taken Hadley to another room to chat, so **Gertrude** didn't get to know much about her. But she did offer to teach **Ernest** how to cut his wife's hair.

Stein is thinking she will take the **Hemingways** up on their offer to come round to their flat and read some of **Ernest's** fiction. He seems to be a good listener. Someone **Gertrude** could easily influence.

❧ FEBRUARY 14, 1922 ❧
HOGARTH HOUSE, RICHMOND, LONDON

About 10 days ago, novelist **Virginia Woolf**, just turned 40 and still recovering from a second bout of influenza, wrote in her diary,

❝ I have taken it into my head that I shan't live till 70…Suppose, I said to myself the other day[,] this pain over my heart wrung me out like a dish cloth & left me dead?…[Last summer I had] two whole months rubbed out."

Now her husband, **Leonard**, 41, has moved her bed downstairs to the living room, which is less lonely for her and more convenient for both of them. She's reading more—*Moby Dick* and a biography of Lord Salisbury—writing a little and receiving visitors. Including her brother-in-law, **Clive Bell**, 40, whom she describes as "all bottom and a little flaxen wig,"

But **Virginia's** temperature has been elevated consistently at 99.5 degrees, and she has been feeling quite competitive with her friend, fellow novelist Katherine Mansfield, 33. The *Saturday Westminster Gazette* is serializing Mansfield's short story "The Garden Party" and a collection of her stories will soon be coming out as a book.

Today, **Virginia** writes in her diary,

❝ K. M. [Mansfield] bursts upon the world in glory next week…I have to hold over [my novel] *Jacob's Room*…til October; & I somehow fear that by that time it will appear to me sterile acrobatics…[I am feeling] all dissipated & invalid-ish…What a 12 months it has been for writing!—& I at the prime of life, with little creatures in my head which won't exist if I don't let them out!"

❧ FEBRUARY 17, 1922 ❧
CLOSERIE DES LILAS,
171 BOULEVARD DU MONTPARNASSE, PARIS

This is a disaster.

French writer and Dada co-founder Andre Breton, about to turn 26, had wanted an evening of intellectual debate among his fellow avant-garde artists and writers on the Left Bank. But just by announcing the "International Congress for the Determination and Defence of the Modern Spirit" last month in the magazine *Comoedia*, he stirred up their passions. So Breton decided that, rather than wait until March as originally planned, he would hold the Congress now, here at the Closerie, one of their favorite cafes.

His so-called friends have turned this evening into a rant against Breton. He had begged Romanian-French poet Tristan Tzara, 25, to bring his followers in the Dada movement along. Tzara refused.

Breton is pleased with the artists who have come: American painter **Man Ray**, 31; French artist Jean Cocteau, 32; Spanish painter Pablo Picasso, 40; Romanian artist Constantin Brancusi, about to turn 46; French composer Erik Satie, 55.

But now they have turned against him—just because he criticized Tzara and Dadaism.

Breton has settled into a regular bourgeois lifestyle. He and his wife of four months have rented a flat that has become a gathering place in the evenings for the avant-garde of Paris. He wants to have philosophical debates—Is a top hat more or less modern than a locomotive, for example—but all these people want to do is scream at each other.

Breton is already planning his next manifesto for *Comoedia* to be titled "After Dada."

❧ FEBRUARY 21, 1922 ❧

70 BIS, RUE NOTRE DAME DES CHAMPS, PARIS

Irish-American lawyer, John Quinn, 51, has been ill recently and this has cut into his time, not only as a successful corporate lawyer, but also as a patron of artists and writers, including Irish novelist James Joyce, 40, living in Paris.

Joyce's controversial novel *Ulysses* has just been published in Paris by an American ex-pat bookstore owner, with financial help from Quinn. He and Shakespeare and Company owner Sylvia Beach, 34, have been tussling with each other in letters. She's always asking for money to support Joyce, and Quinn wonders if the writer really needs that much support. Quinn is sure Beach is getting her share of the profits. Although she has told him that Joyce's royalty is going to be an outstanding 66%.

Recently Beach wrote to Quinn to smooth things over,

 "I know that no matter how testy you like to seem, you are the kindest man alive."

Today, another one of Joyce's American supporters, ex-pat poet Ezra Pound, 36, also living in Paris, is writing one of his usual lengthy and colorful letters, to bring Quinn up to date on the writers he is supporting:

Sylvia Beach

 Cher ami:

> I am sorry you have been ill; has anyone suggested that you work too much. Most men stop when buried, but I see you pushing up the lid of the cercueil, or having a telephone

fixed inside the damn thing ante
mortem, so that you can dictate to
the office...

Joyce told me yesterday that his
english patron [publisher Harriet
Shaw Weaver] had come across with
another $1000, so that his income,
"unearned" (or damn well earned) is
now about £450 per year. So that's
that. I dont think Miss Bitch (as the
name is pronounced by Parisians)
was writing [at Joyce's] instigation...

Ezra Pound *by E. O. Hoppe*

She has been very sporting over
Ulysses, but she is bone ignorant and
lacking in tact. (I mean, in my own
case, that she insults me every other
time I go into the shop, in *perfect*, oh, I am convinced, in perfect
unconsciousness of the fact. She has nothing to gain by insulting me)...

That I think is a fair definition of tactlessness: to insult when you
dont mean to....

I am worried about [poet T. S.] Eliot; and if you start chucking
money about, I shd. certainly make out a case for him, now, before
anyone else...

Eliot came back from his Lausanne specialist looking O.K.; and with
a damn good poem (19 pages) in his suitcase...

[New York publisher Horace] Liveright made a good impression here;
offered to bring out *Ulysses* in the U. S. and hand over 1000 bones to
J. J[oyce]. Why the hell J. J. didn't nail it AT once I don't know. The
terms were o. k. 1000 dollars for first edition, etc...However, Joyce is
off my hands; free, white, 21 years or more, of age etc...

Eliot ought to be private secretary to some rich imbecile...failing that you might send over someone to elope, kidnap, or otherwise eliminate Mrs. E[liot]...

Hell, *mon cher*, will you retire sensibly now? Or will you insist [on] being useful to other people until it is too late?...

So far it has been a winter without colds in the head. Hope to get some Italian sun in April. Have bought lira with that intent, as their value on the exchange seems to be drifting up.

yours ever

Ezra Pound"

Ezra Pound's unique spelling and punctuation have been left intact.

❧ FEBRUARY 25, 1922 ❧
BEFORE DAWN, PRISON SAINT-PIERRE, VERSAILLES, FRANCE

In about 20 seconds, the "Bluebeard of Gambais," Henri Desire Landru, 52, convicted of murdering 11 wealthy women (the police think there were more), walks to the platform, puts his head in the guillotine, says,

❝ I shall be brave,"

and is beheaded, in accordance with his court-ordered sentence.

FYI: The last public execution by guillotine in France was 55 years later in 1977.

✣ MARCH, 1922 ✣
LONDON, OXFORD, PARIS

In newspapers and correspondence in England and France, the reviews are coming in...

❝ No book has ever been more eagerly and curiously awaited by the strange little inner circle of book lovers and litterateurs than James Joyce's *Ulysses*...Mr. James Joyce is a man of genius...I cannot, however, believe that sex plays such a preponderant part in life as Mr. Joyce represents...[Molly Bloom's soliloquy is] the vilest, according to ordinary standards, in all literature...[But] there are phrases in which the words are packed tightly, as trim, as taut, as perfect as these things can be. There are fine ellipses in which a great sweep of meaning is concentrated into a single just right sentence. There is a spot of colour which sets the page aglow...And yet its very obscenity is somehow beautiful and wrings the soul to pity...Has he not exaggerated the vulgarity and magnified the madness of mankind and the mysterious materiality of the universe?"

London Observer, *March 5*

—Sisley Huddleston, *London Observer*

George Slocombe

    " It took, I understand, nearly six years of Mr. Joyce's life to write, and it will take nearly six of ours to read…The book is a staggering feat which, once attempted and more than half achieved, may never be attempted again."

—George Slocombe,
London Daily Herald

    " An Irish Revel: And Some Flappers

Our first impression is that of sheer disgust, our second of irritability because we never know whether a character is speaking or merely thinking, our third of boredom at the continual harping on obscenities (nothing cloys a reader's appetite so quickly as dirt)…Reading Mr. Joyce is like making an excursion into Bolshevist Russia: all standards go by the board…The maddest, muddiest, most loathsome book issued in our own or any other time—inartistic, incoherent, unquotably nasty—a book that one would have thought could only emanate from a criminal lunatic asylum…[Joyce is] the man with the bomb who would blow what remains of Europe into the sky…His intention, so far as he has any social intention, is completely anarchic."

—S. P. B. Mais, *London Daily Express*
letter to a friend in London

✴︎❀✴︎

    " I'm reading the new Joyce—I hate it when I dip here and there, but when I read it in the right order I am much impressed. However I have but read some 30 pages in that order. It has our Irish cruelty and also our kind of strength and the Martello Tower pages are full of beauty. A cruel playful mind like a great soft tiger cat—I hear, as I read, the report of the rebel sergeant in 1898: 'O he was a fine fellow, a fine fellow. It was a pleasure to shoot him.'"

—**William Butler Yeats**, Oxford,
letter to a friend in London

※◦※

" Joyce has a most goddam wonderful book. It'll probably reach you in time. Meantime the report is that he and all his family are starving but you can find the whole crew of them every night in Michaud's where Binney [my wife Hadley] and I can only afford to go about once a week. **Gertrude Stein** says Joyce reminds her of an old woman out in San Francisco. The woman's son struck it rich in the Klondyke and the old woman went around wringing her hands and saying, 'Oh my poor Joey! My poor Joey! He's got so much money!' The damned Irish, they have to moan about something or other, but you never heard of an Irishman starving."

—**Ernest Hemingway**, Paris,
letter to a friend in Chicago

By the end of the month the $12 copies of *Ulysses* have sold out.

❧ AFTER MARCH 3, 1922 ❧
PLAZA HOTEL, NEW YORK CITY, NEW YORK

F. **Scott Fitzgerald**, 25, hopes that his recently launched second novel, *The Beautiful and Damned*, will do at least as well as his first, *This Side of Paradise*, published two years ago.

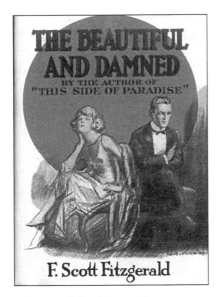

The Beautiful and Damned

Of course this one is based on his relationship with Zelda Sayre, 21, their romance, their marriage. After all, look at the picture on the cover...

But that doesn't mean it's necessarily "blubberingly sentimental" as one early reviewer called it.

Fitzgerald still owes his publisher, Scribner's, almost $6,000, but early sales seem to be going well. He just wasn't prepared for the hostility of some of the critics who had praised him last time.

Scott and Zelda have come to New York for the launch party—well, *parties*, actually—leaving their four-month-old daughter. Scottie, with **Fitzgerald's** parents back in St. Paul, Minnesota, where they have been living for the past year or so.

Scott is excited to be back in Manhattan, but Zelda seems out of sorts.

❧⌘❧

Fitzgerald's classmate from Princeton, critic Edmund "Bunny" Wilson, 26, was quite impressed with *The Beautiful and Damned* when **Scott** asked him to read it in manuscript. But now he is a bit disappointed with the finished product. Who cares about the newlyweds' fights back in Westport, Connecticut, last summer?

When they first arrived back in New York City, Wilson was pleased to see **Scott** and Zelda again. But it has become clear that there is a lot of tension between the two. Motherhood has robbed Zelda, the original "flapper," of a lot of her jazz. Wilson thinks she's looking matronly, and, frankly, fat.

❦

Zelda is pissed off. It's not just that she doesn't want to be pregnant again. **Scott** is totally indifferent to their first child—what will he be like with a second? She's solving that problem with a pill some New York friends have given her.

She's also angry about the way her husband has portrayed her in this new novel. Spoiled brat. Selfish bitch. And to top it off, he has stolen some of *her* writing. Zelda used to enjoy playing the role of muse. But this time **Scott** has used her diaries and letters word for word—there are three pages in the novel labeled "The Diary." It's *her* diary!

Zelda knows one thing for sure. She's not going to have this baby.

❦

On the train from New Haven, Connecticut, into Manhattan, New York City's top columnist, **FPA [Franklin Pierce Adams]**, 40, of the *World* newspaper, is reading his review copy of *The Beautiful and Damned*. He falls asleep.

❧ MARCH 7, 1922 ❧
HOGARTH HOUSE, RICHMOND, LONDON

Virginia Woolf, 40, is watching her husband, **Leonard**, 41, walk their guest for today's tea, fellow novelist Edward Morgan Forster, 43, to the bus stop. Forster is heading out to visit his favorite aunt in Putney, just a few miles away.

Virginia is so pleased that Morgan has come back to England—just last week—after almost a year away in India. But he seems depressed. He's back living with his Mum and cat in Weybridge, in an ugly old house far from a train station and hasn't published a novel in a dozen years.

They discussed their recent mutual discovery of the work of Marcel Proust, 50. Forster started reading him on the boat back home; **Virginia** has been reading the Frenchman while working on a short story, "Mrs. Dalloway in Bond Street." Both admire the way he uses memory to define characters.

Two days ago the **Woolfs** hosted another writer-friend for tea, American ex-pat T. S. Eliot, 34. He too seems a bit distracted by his current situation, working all day in a bank and coming home to a sick wife. **Virginia** has always been intimidated by him. Forster she thinks of as a friend, someone whose opinions she values. Eliot she sees as a competitor.

Tom told them about a long poem, about 40 pages and as yet untitled, that he's working on. He says it is his best work and the **Woolfs'** Hogarth Press has agreed to publication in the fall. He has also received funding to start a quarterly literary magazine, also untitled.

There was something about Eliot that **Virginia** thought she had noticed before. He wears a thin dusting of face powder. Sort of a purplish color. The gossip is that he wants to make himself look even more stressed than he is.

After two months of sickness herself, being bed-ridden and unable to write, **Virginia** is now feeling her energy returning. The doctor has allowed her to get out and walk—which is how she writes, working out the text in her head. And she can now receive guests such as Morgan and Tom.

She still doesn't understand Eliot's enthusiasm for the new novel by Irishman James Joyce, 40, *Ulysses*. **Virginia** and **Leonard** rejected it for their press a few years ago. Now a little bookstore in Paris has published it. The way Eliot talks about the novel, **Virginia** feels that Joyce has done what she is trying to do—maybe even better?

Virginia decides she needs to go back and read *Ulysses* again.

❧ MARCH 10, 1922 ❧
NEW YORK CITY, NEW YORK

Last night *New York Times* drama critic **Alexander Woollcott**, 35, saw the premier of *The Hairy Ape* by Eugene O'Neill, 33, at the Provincetown Playhouse on McDougal Street in Greenwich Village, and his review runs in the paper today:

❝ A bitter, brutal, wildly fantastic play of nightmare hue and nightmare distortion…[The auditorium was] packed to the doors with astonishment…as scene after scene unfolded…[Although the script was] uneven, it seems rather absurd to fret overmuch about the undisciplined imagination of a young playwright towering so conspicuously above the milling mumbling crowd of playwrights who have no imagination at all…A turbulent and tremendous play, so full of blemishes that the merest fledgling among the critics could point out a dozen, yet so vital and interesting and teeming with life that those playgoers who let it escape them will be missing one of the real events of the year."

O'Neill is already established as a playwright, with a Pulitzer Prize under his belt for *Beyond the Horizon*. And another of his plays, *The First Man* just opened a few days ago at The Neighborhood Playhouse in Midtown.

When the Provincetown Playhouse company, which O'Neill has been associated with for the past five years or so, did its first reading of *The Hairy Ape*, he proudly proclaimed,

❝ This is one the bastards [uptown on Broadway] can't do!"

Last night the auditorium was packed and the audience enthusiastic. The lead actor, Louis Wolheim almost 42, got a standing ovation, and there were cries of "Author!"

But O'Neill wasn't in the theatre.

His mother had died while on a trip to the West Coast about a week ago, from a brain tumor, age 64. The opening night of *The Hairy Ape* coincided with the arrival of her body at Grand Central Station. A friend went looking for O'Neill to bring the good news of the play's success. But the hit author was too depressed to be interested.

The two friends spent the night walking around Central Park.

The Hairy Ape

❧ MARCH 13, 1922 ❧
CITY COURTHOUSE, SAN FRANCISCO, CALIFORNIA

Here we go again.

Former film star Roscoe Arbuckle, about to turn 35, is in court for his third trial. There have been two mistrials already, back in December and again last month.

Charges had been brought against him in September after a young actress, Virginia Rappe, 26, died two days after passing out at a Labor Day party Roscoe was attending. He'd tried to help her, but her friends at the party accused him of killing her. Killing?! Roscoe just couldn't believe it. He's a comedian! Not a murderer.

In the second trial, Roscoe's lawyer convinced him to enter into evidence lurid stories about Rappe's past, although Arbuckle felt uncomfortable about that. "Fatty," as his movie character is known, didn't take the stand in his own defense last time. He and his lawyers have decided that this time he will.

One of his loyal friends, Hollywood star Buster Keaton, 26, is in the courtroom to testify in Roscoe's defense. But this past year, one of the prosecution's witnesses, Rappe's friend and Arbuckle's chief accuser, Maud Delmont, 35, a convicted fraudster, has been traveling all over the country giving one-woman shows about the evils of Hollywood. Really.

Arbuckle knows that his once successful career as an actor is over. But he wants to clear his name. He hopes the third time is the charm.

❧ MARCH 15, 1922 ❧
NEW YORK CITY, NEW YORK

Two playwrights from western Pennsylvania, **Marc Connelly**, 31, from McKeesport, and **George S Kaufman**, 32, from Pittsburgh, have a second hit on Broadway. Last year their *Dulcy* with Lynn Fontanne, 34, did well; this season, the three-act comedy *To the Ladies!*, starring Helen Hayes, 21, has been doing even better for the past month at the Liberty Theatre on West 42nd Street.

Helen Hayes and Otto Kruger in To the Ladies!

Truth is, **Connelly** and **Kaufman** finished writing the play just the day before rehearsals started. On opening night, when there were calls for "Author!" they wheeled a mannequin out on to the stage.

The reviews have been good, with most critics preferring it over *Dulcy*. Their Algonquin Hotel lunch buddy **Alexander Woollcott**, 35, wrote in the *New York Times* that *To the Ladies!* provided "an occasion of genuine and quite uproarious jollification."

❧❧

A 10-minute walk away, the first show presented in the Shubert organization's new 49th Street Theatre, the revue *Chauve Souris*, is **Connelly** and **Kaufman's** main competition.

Produced by a troupe originally from Moscow, the evening of songs and sketches is hosted by the Turkish-Russian Nikita Balieff, 49, an émigré from the Bolshevik Revolution, like a lot of the members of his company.

On stage Balieff speaks a combination of broken English, French and Russian while wildly gesticulating, but off stage the theatre world knows that he speaks perfectly good English.

Nikita Balieff

Chauve Souris, or the "flying bat," named for the original variety company Balieff put together back in Russia, has been a touring hit—Paris, London, South Africa. The tune in the show that sends the audience home humming is *The Parade of the Wooden Soldiers*.

Connelly, **Kaufman**, and the other writers they lunch with regularly at the Algonquin are thinking that *Chauve Souris* is ripe for parody.

Today, **Woollcott** has sent a note to **Kaufman** and his wife, publicist Bea Kaufman, 27, on their fifth wedding anniversary:

❝ I have been looking around for an appropriate wooden gift, and am pleased hereby to present you with Elsie Ferguson's performance in her new play."

❧ MID-MARCH, 1922 ❧
39 RUE DESCARTES, PARIS

Toronto Star Weekly foreign correspondent **Ernest Hemingway**, 22, has finished polishing the lead on his article for the paper, "American Bohemians in Paris":

❝ The scum of Greenwich Village, New York, has been skimmed off and deposited in large ladlesful on that section of Paris adjacent to the Café Rotonde. New scum, of course, has risen to take the place of the old, but the oldest scum, the thickest scum and the scummiest scum has come across the ocean, somehow,…and has made the Rotonde the leading Latin Quarter show place for tourists in search of atmosphere."

Ernest and his new wife, Hadley, 30, have been living in Paris since December on his *Toronto Star* salary and her family trust fund. The exchange rate is so favorable that, after they moved from their hotel to a cramped fourth-floor walk-up, he was able to rent this office around the corner, on the top floor of an old hotel where French poet Paul Verlaine died back in the 19th century. **Hemingway** keeps regular writing hours daily.

The editor back in Canada uses almost everything **Ernie** sends, about two articles a week, and he has traveled to Switzerland to file stories about the decline of the tourist trade there, and to Spain to write about tuna fishing.

Finishing up this piece, **Ernest** writes,

❝ The fact that there are 12 francs for a dollar brought over the Rotonders, along with a good many other people, and if the exchange rate goes back to normal they will have to go back to America. They are nearly all loafers expending the energy that an artist puts into his creative work in talking about what they are going to do and condemning the work of all artists who have gained any degree of recognition. By talking about art they obtain the same satisfaction that the real artist does in his work. That is very pleasant, of course, but they insist upon posing as artists."

Next month, the *Toronto Star* is sending **Hemingway** to Italy to cover the Genoa Economic and Financial Conference.

You can read Hemingway's full article here: https://thegrandarchive.wordpress.com/american-bohemians-in-paris-a-weird-lot/

❧ MARCH 21, 1922 ❧
KANDY, CEYLON

HRH Edward, Prince of Wales, 27, is viewing the parade of 200 elephants from the balcony of the Dalada Maligawa, the Glorious Tooth Temple in the complex of the royal palace. The pachyderms walk over white cloths so their feet will never touch the earth. They are accompanied by fireworks and fast-moving Kandyan dancers.

This *perehera*, or procession, is being held in Edward's honor on his state visit as part of his Asian tour of the British colonies. Usually the festival is staged in the summer to celebrate the relic of the Buddha's tooth that is housed within the temple.

HRH Edward, Prince of Wales

To English novelist David Herbert Lawrence, 37, the prince looks tired. "Twitchy…disheartened…badgered about like a doll" he writes to a friend.

Lawrence has been here in Ceylon with his wife, Frieda, 42, for about two weeks, staying with American friends. Kandy has not been the dream paradise he was hoping for. It's hot; it's buggy; he hates the food.

Watching the prince, Lawrence feels empathy; Edward appears lonely, hated by everyone around, with elephants bowing to him.

Lawrence feels they have both been forced to leave their homeland and are being punished here by the heat and the bugs. Edward, just by nature of being a prince; David, for marrying a German wife during the Great War and writing "dirty" novels.

For just a moment, Lawrence feels homesick. He and Frieda have been traveling throughout Europe for the past three years—Italy, Austria, Germany, Sicily, now Ceylon. Maybe it is time to go back.

Kandy Esala perehera

But then David thinks of the pitiful sales his books have in England. And the public response to them.

Keep moving. The next ship out is to Australia. It might at least be cooler.

D. H. Lawrence's experience of the perehera led him to write a poem, "The Elephant Is Slow to Mate," which you can read here. https://poets.org/poem/elephant-slow-mate

❧ MARCH 24, 1922 ❧
FORD MOTOR CO., DETROIT, MICHIGAN

The Ford Motor Co. announces that it will reduce its workweek to 40 hours, five days, eliminating work on weekends.

" Every man needs more than one day a week for rest and recreation. The Ford Co. always has sought to promote ideal home life for its employees. We believe that in order to live properly every man should have more time to spend with his family,"

says Edsel Ford, 28, president.

The entry level pay stays the same, $6 per day, effectively reducing the worker's pay from $36 to $30 per week.

Eleanor and Edsel Ford

❧ LATE MARCH, 1922 ❧
SHAKESPEARE AND COMPANY,
12 RUE DE L'ODEON, PARIS;
31 NASSAU STREET, NEW YORK CITY, NEW YORK;
AND 311 CHATHAM STREET, WINDSOR, ONTARIO

At the Shakespeare and Company bookstore on rue de l'Odeon, the American owner Sylvia Beach, 35, is sending out copies of the new novel *Ulysses*, by Irish ex-pat James Joyce, 40, which she published last month.

Sylvia is able to fill orders from countries all over the world—except the United States.

Because excerpts from the novel, which appeared in *The Little Review* there a few years ago, were determined to be obscene by a New York state court, U.S. Customs officials are on alert.

Oh, she has plenty of orders. One of the largest—25 copies—is from the Washington Square Bookshop in Greenwich Village, where *The Little Review* was first confiscated.

Sylvia is determined. One of Joyce's many benefactors, Irish-American attorney John Quinn, 52, who unsuccessfully argued the case for the *Ulysses* excerpts in court, has suggested smuggling copies in to some northern city from Canada.

Washington Square Bookshop

Sylvia asked one of the young American would-be novelists who frequent her store, **Ernest Hemingway**, 22, if he knew anyone back home in Chicago who could help. The next day he gave Sylvia contact details of a friend and Sylvia shot off a letter to him.

But that was in the beginning of February. She didn't hear anything until last week when he sent a brief telegram:

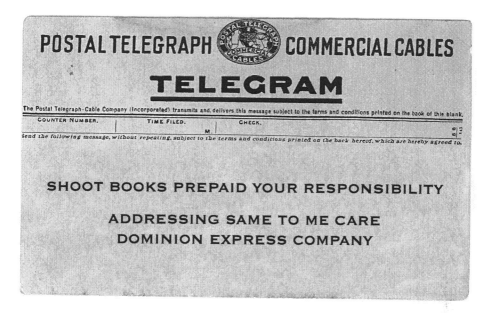

with a Canadian address.

Not very promising.

Sylvia is thinking of giving up on **Hemingway's** friend and exploring one of Quinn's contacts, a good friend of his, Mitchell Kennerley, 43, who has a successful Park Avenue auction house. Kennerley imports books and other items from the UK all the time. Quinn says Mitch is friends with the captain of a transatlantic liner who could bring *Ulysses* over from London, slowly, in batches of 25 or 30 copies per month.

That might be the best option.

In his law office, John Quinn is catching up on his correspondence. He is updating Sylvia Beach on the fate of *Ulysses* in New York. Copies have started to appear in bookshops here. One of his favorites, Drake's on 40th Street, is selling her $12 non-deluxe copies for $20; Brentano's for $35, even $50.

How did they get a hold of the books?! Traveling Americans might have brought them back in their luggage. But Quinn advises Sylvia that the authorities will soon start confiscating any that they find. Some returning tourists have already had their copies destroyed at the Port of New York.

Quinn is willing to make an arrangement with Kennerley.

Beach would have to ship the books in large quantities from Paris to London. They would enter the U. S. as freight, so customs would probably overlook them; they are more intent these days on catching bootleggers. Even if the books were found, they would probably be returned to London rather than burned.

Kennerley would collect the cash from the American buyers, have the copies delivered by private carriers—thereby avoiding sending "obscene" material through the mail—and pass the profits on to Sylvia. Retaining a commission of 10% of the retail price.

Quinn emphasizes to her that Kennerley is willing to break the law and, if he were arrested,

❝ There wouldn't be a ghost of a shade of a shadow of a chance of acquitting Kennerly."

In fact, Quinn tells her, hold on to the 14 copies he ordered for now, until he comes up with a definitive plan to receive them.

In Windsor, Ontario, Barnet Braverman, 34, is wondering why he hasn't heard anything from that American woman in Paris who wants him to smuggle books across the border.

When her initial letter finally caught up to him a week or so ago—he had moved from Chicago to Toronto and is now packing to move to Detroit—he was intrigued.

Miss Beach said a mutual friend had recommended him and that she needs to get copies of James Joyce's new novel, *Ulysses*, to Americans—particularly New York publishers like Knopf and Huebsch who are too yellow to publish it themselves.

Braverman really wants to have a part in sticking it to the publishing establishment. His new ad agency job here in Windsor means he will be taking a short ferry ride from and to Detroit across Lake St. Clair every day as part of his commute.

Barnet is thinking he should write Miss Beach a detailed letter so she knows how eager he is to help out.

❧ MARCH 30, 1922 ❧
THE NEW AGE MAGAZINE, LONDON

A piece by American poet Ezra Pound, 36, currently living in Paris, titled "Credit and the Fine Arts: A Practical Application," appears in *The New Age* magazine:

> " [Democracy] has signally failed to provide for its best writers…That is to say, the worst work usually brings the greatest financial reward… We can't expect illiterate, newly rich millionaires to pay for things they have not the taste to enjoy."

Pound goes on to outline his proposed scheme to collect small donations from subscribers to fund 20 or 30 writers "who have definitely proved they have something in them and are capable of expression." The best gift to an artist "is leisure in which to work," he writes.

Then Pound makes clear to the reader who he has in mind:

> " Rightly or wrongly some of us consider [poet T. S.] Eliot's employment in a bank the worst waste in contemporary literature. During his recent three-months' absence due to complete physical breakdown, he produced a very important sequence of poems: one of the few things in contemporary literature to which one can ascribe permanent value."

Pound makes it clear that the wishes of Mr. Eliot "have *not* been consulted."

Ezra and his wife then leave to go on vacation in Italy.

❧ APRIL 3, 1922 ❧
BILTMORE HOTEL, 271 WEST 47TH STREET, NEW YORK CITY, NEW YORK

Happy second wedding anniversary to popular novelist **F. Scott Fitzgerald**, 25, and his lovely bride, Zelda, 22.

They are celebrating with yet another party, this time at the Biltmore where they spent their honeymoon.

In New York for the past few weeks for publication of **Scott's** second novel, *The Beautiful and Damned*, the **Fitzgeralds** are now preparing to go back to his hometown, St. Paul, Minnesota, and their five-month old daughter, Scottie, who has been staying with his family.

There has been a lot to celebrate. **Scott** is trying

Biltmore Hotel advertisement

his hand at playwrighting, spending the last few months writing *The Vegetable: From Postman to President*, which he is convinced will make him rich for life.

Fitzgerald has sold the movie rights to *The Beautiful and Damned* to Warner Brothers for $2,500. Although he thinks that's an awfully small price.

Sales of the novel are going well. There have been some negative reviews, but the most positive one appeared in the *New York Tribune* yesterday—by Zelda.

In "Friend Husband's Latest," she pronounced the book "absolutely perfect"; the character based on her, "most amusing"; and urged readers to buy the book because she will get a platinum ring and the "cutest" $300 gold-cloth gown. The only thing that bothers Zelda is that her old diary has disappeared and some passages in the novel sound awfully familiar. She figures "friend husband" believes that "plagiarism begins at home."

Ha ha. Except that Zelda isn't kidding. And she isn't pregnant anymore.

❧ EARLY APRIL, 1922 ☙
SAM HARRIS THEATRE, 226 WEST 42ND STREET, NEW YORK CITY, NEW YORK

Once again, Essie Goode Robeson, 26, has convinced her husband of less than a year, Columbia law student Paul, about to turn 24, to take a break from his studies and appear in a play.

Paul Robeson in Taboo

Taboo opened here a few nights ago. Written by Mary Hoyt Wiborg, 34 ("Hoytie" to her posh family), now living in Paris, the play is set before the Civil War on a Louisiana plantation and in Africa. The star, English actress Margaret Wycherly, 40, is the only white actor in the cast.

Paul accepted the part reluctantly. He is worried about the effect this might have on his grades at Columbia, where he is doing well. Although, Essie was right the last time she convinced him to appear in a new play, *Simon the Cyrenian*, back before they were married.

This time, Essie has come to every rehearsal to take notes and give him advice about how to improve his performance. She is convinced that, even with a Columbia law degree, it is going to be difficult for a Black man to get a good job. Paul has received good reviews so far, and, with his talent for acting and singing, Essie figures that at least he will have something to fall back on.

❧ APRIL, 1922 ❧
ENGLAND, AMERICA, FRANCE, AND IRELAND

Comment continues to come in reacting to the new novel *Ulysses*, by Irishman James Joyce, 40, published two months ago by a small bookshop in Paris, Shakespeare and Company, owned by American ex-pat Sylvia Beach, 35.

❝ **SCANDAL OF JAMES JOYCE'S *ULYSSES***

After a rather boresome [sic] perusal of James Joyce's *Ulysses*, published in Paris for private subscribers at the rate of three guineas in francs, I can realize one reason at least for Puritan America's Society for the Prevention of Vice, and can understand why the Yankee judges fined the publishers of *The Little Review* $100 for the publication of a very rancid chapter of the Joyce stuff, which appears to have been written by a perverted lunatic who has made a specialty of the literature of the latrine...

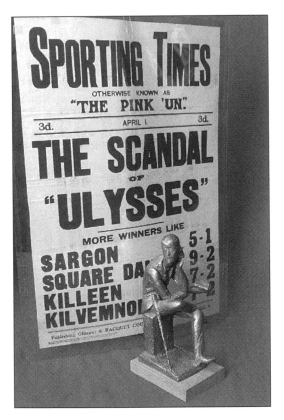

Sporting Times

Joyce is a writer of talent, but in *Ulysses* he has ruled out all the elementary decencies of life and dwells appreciatively on things that sniggering louts of schoolboys guffaw about...There are whole chapters of it without any punctuation or other guide to what the writer is really getting at. Two-thirds of it is incoherent, and the passages that are plainly written are devoid of wit, displaying only a coarse salacrity [sic] intended for humour...The main contents of the book are enough to make a Hottentot sick...[However] there are quite a number of the New York intelligentsia who declare that Joyce has written the best book in the world."

> —"Aramis," *Sporting Times*, England

❝ [Joyce is] Rabelais after a nervous breakdown."

> —*Sheffield Daily Telegraph*, England

❝ [*Ulysses*] has nothing at all to do with Homer...The book itself in its blue paper cover looks at first glance like nothing so much as a telephone directory...It seems a pity that Mr. Joyce, who might be a universally admired writer, restricts the appeal of his work by so many Zolaesque expressions, which are, to say the least, disfiguring."

> —"Diary of a Man About Town," *London Evening News*

❝ [Joyce is] an intensely serious man [with] the mind of an artist, abnormally sensitive to the secret of individuality of emotions and things...A genius of the very highest order, strictly comparable to Goethe or Dostoevsky...*Ulysses* is, fundamentally (though it is much else besides), an immense, a prodigious self-laceration, the tearing away from himself, by a half-demented man of genius, of inhibitions and limitations which have grown to be flesh of his flesh...[Joyce] is the man with the bomb who would blow what remains of Europe into the sky...This transcendental buffoonery, this sudden uprush of

the *vis comica* into a world where in the tragic incompatibility of the
practical and the instinctive is embodied, is a very great achievement."

—"Mr. Joyce's *Ulysses*," John Middleton Murry,
Nation and Athenaeum, England

" [Joyce's vision of human nature is] mean, hostile, and uncharitable,...
He is sometimes dazzlingly original. If he does not see life whole
he sees it piercingly. His ingenuity is marvelous. He has wit. He has
a prodigious humor. He is afraid of naught...It is more indecent,
obscene, scatological, and licentious than the majority of professedly
pornographic books...He says everything—everything...The code
is smashed to bits...I have never read anything to surpass [Molly
Bloom's soliloquy], and I doubt if I have ever read anything to equal
it...[Joyce] apparently thinks that there is something truly artistic
and high minded in playing the lout to the innocent and defenceless
reader...He has made novel reading into a fair imitation of penal
servitude. Many persons could not continue reading *Ulysses*; they
would be obliged, by mere shock, to drop it."

—"James Joyce's *Ulysses*," Arnold Bennett,
Outlook, England

" Amused, stimulated, charmed, interested (through the first three chapters
only to be) puzzled, bored, irritated, & disillusioned as by a queasy
undergraduate scratching his pimples (by the end of chapter six)...It
was an illiterate, underbred book (by a) self-taught working man"

—**Virginia Woolf**, in her diary, England

※

" [*Ulysses* is] a step toward making the modern world possible for
art. [It gives] a shape and a significance to the immense panorama
of futility and anarchy which is contemporary history...[Joyce has

replaced narrative with] the mythical method…[It is] a book to which we are all indebted and from which none of us can escape."

—T. S. Eliot, "*Ulysses*, Order and Myth," *The Dial*, America

❦

❝ [Molly Bloom's soliloquy is a feat of] diabolic clairvoyance, black magic."

—Paris edition of *New York Herald*, France

❝ Take this Irishman Joyce, a sort of Zola gone to seed. Someone recently sent me a copy of *Ulysses*. I was told I must read it, but how can one plow through such stuff? I read a little here and there, but, oh my God! How bored I got! Probably Joyce thinks that because he prints all the dirty little words he is a great novelist. You know, of course, he got his ideas from Dujardin?…Joyce, Joyce, why he's nobody…from the Dublin docks: no family, no breeding. Someone else once sent me his *A Portrait of the Artist as a Young Man*, a book entirely without style or distinction; why, I did the same thing, but much better in

George Moore *by Edouard Manet*

The Confessions of a Young Man. Why attempt the same thing unless you can turn out a better book?…*Ulysses* is hopeless, it is absurd to imagine that any good end can be served by trying to record every single thought and sensation of any human being. That's not art, that's attempting to copy the London Directory…He lives here in Paris, I understand. How does he manage to make a living? His books don't sell. Maybe he has money?"

—**George Moore**, in conversation in France

66 A welter of pornography (the rudest school-boy kind), and unformed and unimportant drivel."

—Edith Wharton, France

66 It bursted over us like an explosion in print, whose words and phrases fell upon us like a gift of tongues, like a less than holy Pentecostal experience"

—Young American in France

꧁꧂

66 I should think you would need something to restore your self-respect after this last inspection of the stinkpots…Everything dirty seems to have the same irresistible attraction for you that cow-dung has for flies."

—The author's brother, Stanislaus Joyce, Ireland

66 I've always told him he should give up writing and take up singing."

—The author's partner, Nora Barnacle,
visiting her mother in Ireland

❧ APRIL **12, 1922** ❧
CITY COURTHOUSE, SAN FRANCISCO, CALIFORNIA

The jury is returning after only six minutes. Former film star Roscoe "Fatty" Arbuckle, 35, stands to hear the amazingly swift verdict.

The foreperson announces that they have unanimously found Arbuckle not guilty—after two previous mistrials—in the death of actress Virginia Rappe, 26, two days after a party in a local hotel last September.

The coroner had found no evidence of rape; the autopsy had shown no evidence of violence. Virginia had been seriously ill from too much bathtub alcohol. But it might have been Arbuckle's own testimony which swayed them this time.

The jury had come to their conclusion in exactly one minute.

The additional five minutes were spent drafting a formal apology to Arbuckle, which the foreman now reads:

❝ Acquittal is not enough for Roscoe Arbuckle. We feel that a great injustice has been done him. We feel also that it was only our plain duty to give him this exoneration, under the evidence, for there was not the slightest proof adduced to connect him in any way with the commission of a crime. He was manly throughout the case and told a straightforward story on the witness stand, which we all believed. The happening at the hotel was an unfortunate affair for which Arbuckle, so the evidence shows, was in no way responsible. We wish him success and hope that the American people will take the judgment of 14 men and women who have sat listening for 31 days to evidence, that Roscoe Arbuckle is entirely innocent and free from all blame."

All 12 jury members and two alternates shake Arbuckle's hand and embrace him. Then they all pose for pictures together.

Now Roscoe has to figure out how to pay his lawyers the $700,000 he owes them for their services during three trials over eight months.

❧ APRIL **14, 1922** ❧
SCRIBNER'S, 153-157 FIFTH AVENUE, NEW YORK CITY, NEW YORK

This is a very different letter that Max Perkins, 37, editor at Scribner's publishing house, is getting ready to write.

Usually, he's writing letters of encouragement to his authors, like hit novelist **F. Scott Fitzgerald**, 25.

This letter is personal.

Earlier this month he and his wife Louise, 34, met a private school music and dance teacher from Middleburg, Virginia, Elizabeth Lemmon, 28, on her annual visit to her family in Plainfield, New Jersey.

Elizabeth, who also manages a local baseball team in Virginia, left quite an impression on Max. He has been looking for a reason to write to her and found that she had left behind a few cigarettes. He writes,

❝ Dear Miss Lemon [Max is a terrible speller]:—When I found these cigarettes you had left I thought at first to keep them as a remembrance. But I am far from needing a remembrance. I then recalled that you had said you meant to stop smoking because cigarettes of this brand were no longer made & I thought I must save you from that dreadful heart-broken feeling you have when you don't smoke…*Next* year [when you visit], please remember I sent these and thank me. And I now thank you for all the pleasure you gave me—& I suppose, everyone else in the neighborhood—by being here this year.

Maxwell Perkins

P.S. [I have always liked Virgil's phrase] 'and she revealed herself to be a goddess.' But I never really knew its meaning till I saw you coming toward me through our hall the other night."

❧ EASTER, 1922 ❧
THOOR BALLYLEE, COUNTY GALWAY;
DOMINICK STREET, GALWAY CITY;
AND RUTLAND SQUARE, DUBLIN

Irish poet and playwright **William Butler Yeats**, 56, and his family are settling in nicely to their new country home in the west of Ireland. Well, not a traditional "country home." A Norman tower, actually. Which **Yeats** has renamed Thoor Ballylee.

From the top of his tower he can see the Aughty Mountains to the east and the hills of the Burren to the West.

Thoor Ballylee

He writes to friends,

❝ All we can see from our windows is beautiful and quiet…Everything is so beautiful that to go elsewhere is to leave beauty behind."

❧❧

Yet, about 20 miles away in Galway City, Nora Barnacle, 38, home from Paris on a family visit, is staying in her uncle's house with her two children, Giorgio, 16, and Lucia, 14.

Insurgents from the Irish Republican Army (IRA), fighting against the right of the newly declared Irish Free State to uphold the Anglo-Irish Treaty, burst into the house.

They demand to use the bedroom as a base to fire on their enemies out the window.

Nora is appalled. And panicked. Her partner, the father of their children, Irish novelist James Joyce, 40, had begged her to not come here. He knows there is a Civil War raging throughout the country and he fears for their safety. He has been writing her anguished letters from their home in Paris ever since she left:

66 I am like a man looking into a dark pool."

She and the children arrived a few weeks ago, coming over via London, which Nora really enjoyed. She might try to convince Jim to move there, rather than continue to live in Paris. At least they'd be surrounded by the English language.

But right now, Nora is thinking that she needs to get herself and her kids on a train to Dublin as fast as she can.

⁂

Michael Collins, 31, recently named Chair of the Provisional Government of the pro-Treaty Irish Free State, gets out of his car at Vaughan's Hotel, followed by other members of the National Army. A group of 12 armed, anti-government IRA men rush by him and start shooting at his entourage. Collins fires at them with his revolver and disarms one of the younger men. The boy admits he didn't realize that he had just shot at the leader of the Irish Free State. Good thing he missed.

My thanks to Rena McAllen, member of the board of directors of the Yeats Thoor Ballylee Society, for assistance with details of Thoor Ballylee, and Neil Weatherall, author of the play, The Passion of the Playboy Riots, *for assistance with details of the Irish Civil War.*

❧ MID-APRIL, 1922 ❧
MONK'S HOUSE, RODMELL, EAST SUSSEX, ENGLAND

Novelist **Virginia Woolf**, 40, is sitting in a comfy chair in the **Woolfs'** house in the country with a blue-bound book in her lap.

Virginia is s l o w l y cutting each page of the brand-new copy of *Ulysses* which she ordered from her London bookseller. £4. Not cheap.

She knows she has to actually *read* the book, not just handle it. She did read the first eight chapters earlier this year, in magazine excerpts. And then re-read the first four.

Then put it down and told herself she would definitely finish it. Soon.

Her husband **Leonard**, 41, jumped right in and started reading. Ironically, the manuscript of *Ulysses* was submitted to them a few years ago, to be published by their own Hogarth Press. They declined. Too big a print job, they explained.

Virginia has written to her brother-in-law, art critic **Clive Bell**, also 40:

❝ Mr. Joyce…I have him on the table…**Leonard** is already 30 pages deep…I look, and sip, and shudder."

After all, she's been ill. Bad case of the flu. And, despite that, she has been working on a long short story—"Mrs. Dalloway in Bond Street"—that she might send to their friend, American ex-pat Tom Eliot, 33, for his new magazine. If she has it done in a few weeks.

Eliot is one of the those who has been praising Joyce and his latest book. Sometimes **Virginia** thinks Eliot likes everyone else's writing better than hers.

She'll start reading it again if the rain keeps up.

AFTER EASTER, 1922
HERTFORD COLLEGE, OXFORD; AND
TRINITY COLLEGE, CAMBRIDGE, ENGLAND

Evelyn Waugh, 19, is absolutely over the moon to be back on campus at Oxford.

Waugh has just been at home in Hampstead, London, with his father for Easter vacation. He thought he'd go mad with the boredom.

Having won a scholarship late last year, Evelyn entered Hertford College in January. Starting halfway through the academic year put him somewhat at a disadvantage; all the other first-years have been making friends since their arrival last September.

Despite this awkward timing, Waugh has been fitting into campus life quite well. He smokes a pipe; he rides a bike. He is writing for both college magazines, *Cherwell* and *Isis*, and has given his maiden speech at the Oxford Union. He chose to oppose the motion,

" This House would welcome Prohibition."

However, one of the other disadvantages of his late start was that all the good rooms had been taken and Evelyn is left with a tiny, dark, ground floor chamber next to the buttery.

This location makes it a natural stopover for the campus drunks, day and night. The other evening, an inebriated member of the Bullingdon club vomited into Waugh's window.

About 90 miles northeast, at Trinity College, Cambridge, Russian émigré Vladimir Nabokov, about to turn 23, is returning to campus for his final term. He is not in good spirits. Spring always makes him think of past years spent with his family in the Russian countryside, before they were forced by the Bolshevik Revolution to go into exile.

And less than a month ago, his father, V. D. Nabokov, 52, was assassinated by two Russian monarchists at a political conference in Berlin. They were aiming at another politician; Vlad's Dad tried to shield him and was shot twice.

Hertford College Bridge, Oxford

Despite his melancholy, Vlad is determined to pass his final exams and graduate in June. He is going to throw himself into studying and not allow any diversions.

However, one of his fellow Russian students has just come into his room with a novel he has discovered, *Ulysses*, and he is reading out incredible passages from some raunchy woman's soliloquy.

✣ APRIL, 1922 ✣

VANITY FAIR MAGAZINE, NEW YORK CITY, NEW YORK

American writer Djuna Barnes, 29, arrived in Paris a few months ago with a letter of introduction to one of the ex-patriate writers she most admires, James Joyce, 40. This month, her profile of the Irishman appears in *Vanity Fair* magazine.

A PORTRAIT OF THE MAN WHO IS, AT PRESENT, ONE OF THE MORE SIGNIFICANT FIGURES IN LITERATURE

BY DJUNA BARNES

" …Of Joyce, the man, one has heard very little. I had seen a photograph of him, the collar up about the narrow throat, the beard, heavier in those days, descending into the abyss of the hidden bosom. I had been told that he was going blind, and we in America learned from Ezra Pound that 'Joyce is the only man on the continent who continues to produce in spite of poverty and sickness, working from eight to 16 hours a day.'…

And then, one day, I came to Paris. Sitting in the café of the Deux Magots, that faces the little church of St. Germain des Près, I saw approaching, out of the fog and damp, a tall man, with head slightly lifted and slightly turned, giving to the wind an orderly distemper of red and black hair, which descended sharply into a scant wedge on an out-thrust chin.

He wore a blue grey coat, too young it seemed, partly because he had thrust its gathers behind him, partly because the belt which circled it, lay two full inches above the hips…

Because he had heard of the suppression of *The Little Review* on account of *Ulysses* and of the subsequent trial, he sat down opposite me, who was familiar with the whole story, ordering a white wine.

He began to talk at once. 'The pity is,'
he said, seeming to choose his words for
their age rather than their aptness, 'the
public will demand and find a moral in my
book—or worse they may take it in some
more serious way, and on the honor of a
gentleman, there is not one single serious
line in it.'

For a moment there was silence. His hands,
peculiarly limp in the introductory shake
and peculiarly pulpy,...lay, one on the stem
of the glass, the other, forgotten, palm out,
on the most delightful waistcoat it has ever

James Joyce

been my happiness to see. Purple with alternate doe and dog heads...

He saw my admiration and he smiled. 'Made by the hand of my
grandmother for the first hunt of the season' and there was another
silence in which he arranged and lit a cigar...

'In *Ulysses* I have recorded, simultaneously, what a man says, sees,
thinks, and what such seeing, thinking, saying does, to what you
Freudians call the subconscious,—but as for psychoanalysis.' he
broke off, 'it's neither more nor less than blackmail.'

He raised his eyes. There is something unfocused in them,—the same
paleness seen in plants long hidden from the sun,—and sometimes a
little jeer that goes with a lift and rounding of the upper lip...

If I were asked what seemed to be the most characteristic pose of
James Joyce I should say that of the head; turned farther away than
disgust and not so far as death,...—think of him as a heavy man
yet thin, drinking a thin cool wine with lips almost hidden in his
high narrow head, or smoking the eternal cigar, held slightly above
shoulder-level, and never moved until consumed, the mouth brought
to and taken away from it to eject the sharp jets of yellow smoke...

It has been my pleasure to talk to him many times during my four months in Paris. We have talked of rivers and religion, of the instinctive genius of the church which chose, for the singing of its hymns, the voice without 'overtones'—the voice of the eunuch. We have talked of women, about women he seems a bit disinterested. Were I vain I should say he is afraid of them, but I am certain he is only a little skeptical of their existence. We have talked of Ibsen, of Strindberg, Shakespeare. '*Hamlet* is a great play, written from the standpoint of the ghost,' and of Strindberg, 'No drama behind the hysterical raving.'

We have talked of death, of rats, of horses, the sea; languages, climates and offerings. Of artists and of Ireland...

Sometimes his wife, Nora, and his two children have been with him. Large children, almost as tall as he is himself, and Nora walks under fine red hair, speaking with a brogue that carries the dread of Ireland in it; Ireland as a place where poverty has become the art of scarcity. A brogue a little more defiant than Joyce's which is tamed by preoccupation.

Joyce has few friends, yet he is always willing to leave his writing table and his white coat of an evening, to go to some quiet near-by cafe, there to discuss anything that is not 'artistic' or 'flashy' or 'new.' Callers have often found him writing in the night, or drinking tea with Nora. I myself once came upon him as he lay full length on his stomach poring over a valise full of notes taken in his youth for *Ulysses*...

However it is with him, he will come away for the evening, for he is simple, a scholar, and sees nothing objectionable in human beings if they will only remain in place..."

❧ APRIL 22, 1922 ❧
2:30 PM, PICCADILLY CIRCUS, LONDON

On the birthday of his older brother John, who was killed at the end of the Great War, Martin Bateson, 22, son of renowned Cambridge University biologist William, 60, and older brother of Gregory, 17, his girlfriend having recently rejected the play he wrote about their relationship,

Piccadilly Circus

walks up to the Eros statue, puts a white glove on his right hand, takes a .25 caliber automatic pistol out of his pocket, places it next to his right ear, and pulls the trigger.

❧ APRIL, 1922 ❧
PALAZZO SAN GIORGIO, GENOA, ITALY; AND
50 GORDON SQUARE, BLOOMSBURY, LONDON

The Genoa Economic and Financial Conference is underway.

British Prime Minister David Lloyd George, 59, instigated this conference of delegates from selected European countries, to plan for the "reconstruction of economic Europe, devastated and broken into fragments by the desolating agency of war," as he told the UK House of Commons. They gave him a rousing vote of confidence.

Over 700 journalists applied for the 200 ticketed slots to cover the four-week get together. Some of them have to sit on the floor.

The correspondent for the *Toronto Star*, American **Ernest Hemingway**, 22, arrived early in the month and began filing stories. His first description of the setting:

> Genoa is crowded, a modern Babel with a corps of perspiring interpreters trying to bring the representatives of 40 [sic] different countries together. The narrow streets flow with crowds kept orderly by thousands of Italian troops."

The troops in their black fezzes are visible to discourage violent outbreaks by Communists or anti-Communists in this city which is one-third "Red." The best way to keep the peace seems to be closing the cafes, **Hemingway** observes.

The tension is exacerbated by Britain's insistence, over France's objection, that both Germany and Soviet Russia attend. France doesn't want to invite their main debtor, the Weimar Republic, nor any representatives of the new Bolshevik government in Moscow.

America has declined to participate at all.

Living in Paris with his new wife since late last year, **Ernie** is happy to be covering his first major political event for the *Star*. He is getting used to filing his copy by cable, and a few of the more experienced journalists here have given him some tips. Muckraking investigative reporter Lincoln Steffens, just turned 56, showed him how to run words together—"aswellas"—to save money. **Hemingway** loves this.

❝ It's wonderful! It's a new language. No fat, all bones and structure,"

he exclaims to his colleagues over chianti.

During the opening ceremony, the arrival of Lloyd George is met with a loud ovation. The other delegations enter, and, as **Hemingway** describes the scene:

❝ When the hall is nearly full, the British delegation enters. They have come in motor cars through the troop-lined streets and enter with elan. They are the best dressed delegation...The hall is crowded and sweltering and the four empty chairs of the Soviet delegation are the four emptiest looking chairs I have ever seen. Everyone is wondering whether they will not appear. Finally they come through the door and start making their way through the crowd. Lloyd George looks at them intently, fingering his glasses...A mass of secretaries follow the Russian delegates, including two girls with fresh faces, hair bobbed in the fashion started by [American dancer] Irene Castle, and modish tailored suits. They are far and away the best-looking girls in the conference hall. The Russians are seated. Someone hisses for silence, and Signor Facta starts the dreary round of speeches that sends the conference under way."

❦❦❦

Economist **John Maynard Keynes**, 38, is one of the many Brits attending. He represented his government in Versailles at the Paris Peace Conference three years ago—when Germany and Russia were definitely not invited. But now he is here as General Editor of a special 12-part series, "Reconstruction in Europe" by the *Manchester Guardian Commercial*. These supplements are being translated into five languages and will include contributions from leading statesmen and businessmen, along with 13 pieces by **Keynes**.

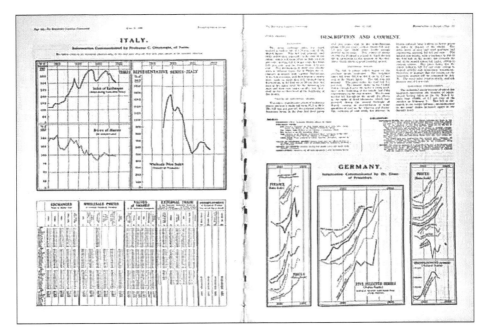

Graphs in Manchester Guardian *supplement*

The Manchester Guardian approached **Maynard** last year to take on this role, and he agreed only when they assured him he would be able to closely supervise the writers who would be chosen. **Keynes** is using this medium to get across his opinions of the steps being taken to rebuild a Europe which has been so devastated by the Great War.

Throughout the conference, **Keynes** keeps up a steady correspondence with his friends back home. Particularly his most recent lover, Russian ballerina Lydia Lopokova, 30.

Back in Bloomsbury, Lydia is enjoying settling into her new home in 50 Gordon Square, where **Maynard** installed her before he left, surrounded by his artsy Bloomsbury friends and just a few doors away from his residence in number 46.

Lydia has left the Ballets Russes, where she was a principal dancer for many years, and is now dancing in Covent Garden with the company led by fellow Russian Leonid Massine, 25, former choreographer with the Ballets Russes.

Since **Maynard** left for Italy, Lydia has been writing to him almost every day about the details of her new London life; commenting on his articles in the *Guardian—*

❝   Your expression in the end give me nice tremblings"

—and how much she misses him—

❝   I place melodious strokes all over you. **Maynard**, you are very nice."

Thanks to Dr. Marie Hooper for assistance in understanding European history.

❧ APRIL **26, 1922** ❧
WEYBRIDGE, SURREY, ENGLAND; AND
PORT SAID, EGYPT

The poem "Ghosts" by J. R. Ackerley, 25, in the recent issue of the *London Mercury* magazine, has moved English novelist Edward Morgan Forster, 43, so much that he is writing a letter to the author.

The haunting first lines,

> **"** Can they still live,
> Beckon and cry
> Over the years
> After they die…
> Are they distressed
> If we forget
> After they've perished?..."

remind him of his lover,
Mohammed el Adl, 22, who
is dying at home in Port Said,
Egypt.

On Morgan's journey back from
India last month, he stopped
over in Port Said, and they spent
a memorable month together.
But Mohammed was so ill with
tuberculosis, it was clear to
Forster that they would not see
each other again.

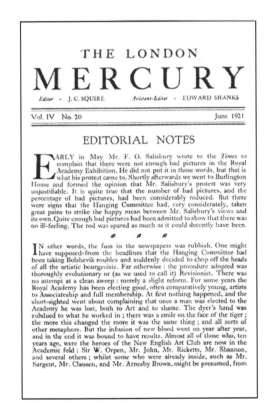

London Mercury

The poem goes on:

   Softly they stole,
Wave upon wave,
Into his grave…
'You will forget…
'You will forget…'"

Morgan pours out his feelings in a long letter to the poet Ackerley, whom he has never met. He has always felt that it is easier to write to strangers.

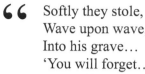

In Port Said, Mohammed's illness is worsening, and he is writing a brief letter to his lover back in England.

   dear Morgan,

I am sending you the photogh
I am very bad
I got nothing more
to say
the family are good
my compliment
to [your] mother
my love to you
my love to you
my love to you
do not forget your
ever friend

Moh el Adl."

❧ APRIL **30**, **1922** ❧
49TH STREET THEATRE, 235 WEST 49TH STREET, NEW YORK CITY, NEW YORK

You've seen them in the speakeasies of Manhattan…

You've seen them lunching at the Algonquin Hotel…

Now see them on stage in…

No Sirree!
49th Street Theatre

Now playing…For one night only!

Produced by Frank Case, manager of the Algonquin Hotel

Programme

Your host for the evening,

"The Spirit of American Drama,"

played by **Heywood Broun**

Music provided throughout the evening offstage (and off-key) by Jascha Heifetz

"The Opening Chorus"

Performed by **Franklin Pierce Adams [FPA]**, **Robert Benchley**, **Marc Connelly**, **George S Kaufman**, John Peter Toohey, **Alexander Woollcott**, (Dressed only in their bathrobes)

"The Editor Regrets"

(In which poet Dante has his first writing rejected by *Droll Tales* magazine)

Performed by Mary Brandon, **Marc Connelly**, Donald Ogden Stewart and others

"The Filmless Movies"

Featuring **Franklin Pierce Adams [FPA]** and, on piano, Baron Ireland

(composer of "If I Had of Knew What I'd Ought to Have Knew, I'd Never Had Did What I Done)

"The Greasy Hag: A Eugene O'Neill Play in One Act"

(Setting to be determined by the audience)

Agitated Seamen played by **Marc Connelly**, **George S Kaufman** and **Alexander Woollcott**

The Murdered Woman played by Ruth Gilmore

(Please be advised there will be strong language)

"He Who Gets Flapped"

Performed by Robert Sherwood

Featuring "The Everlasting Ingenue Blues,"

Music by Deems Taylor, lyrics by **Dorothy Parker**

Performed by the chorus, Tallulah Bankhead, Mary Brandon, Ruth Gilmore, Helen Hayes, Mary Kennedy and others

"Between the Acts"

The Manager and the Manager's Brother played by Brock and Murdock Pemberton

"Big Casino Is Little Casino: The Revenge of One Who Has Suffered"

By **George S Kaufman**

(who advises the audience,
"The idea has been to get square with
everybody in three two-minute acts.")

"Mr. Whim Passes By— An A. A. Milne Play"

Performed by Helen Hayes and others

"Kaufman and Connelly from the West"

Performed by **George S Kaufman** and **Marc Connelly**

("Oh, we are **Kaufman** and **Connelly** from Pittsburgh,

We're **Kaufman** and **Connelly** from the West…")

"Zowie or The Curse of an Aking Heart"

Featuring Dregs, a butler, played by **Alexander Woollcott**

And finally…

"The Treasurer's Report"

By **Robert Benchley**

Featuring the last-minute substitute for the treasurer, played by **Robert Benchley**

Immediately following the programme, all cast and audience members are invited to the nearby digs of Herbert Bayard and Maggie Swope

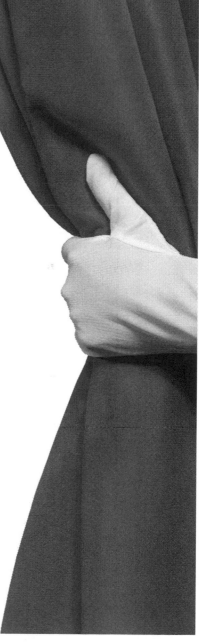

❧ APRIL THROUGH MAY, 1922 ❧
HOGARTH HOUSE, RICHMOND; TIDMARSH, BERKSHIRE;
AND GARSINGTON, OXFORDSHIRE, ENGLAND

April. Novelist **Virginia Woolf**, 40, writes to her friend, Lady Ottoline Morrell, 48, to arrange a visit to the Morrell's country home, Garsington. **Virginia** suggests the last weekend in May, writing,

> ❝ It's such an age since I was at Garsington, and it never seems to me a house on the ground like other houses, but a caravan, a floating palace."

April. Ottoline writes to her friend, novelist Edward Morgan Forster, 43, just back from India, inviting him to Garsington for the last weekend in May, telling him that **Virginia** as well as American ex-pat poet T. S. Eliot, 33, are invited for that weekend also.

Mid-May. Forster responds to Ottoline's invitation, saying that he can't come that weekend because he will be visiting their mutual friend, writer **Lytton Strachey**, 42, in Tidmarsh, Berkshire, where **Lytton** is renting a house owned by economist **John Maynard Keynes**, 38. Forster apologizes to Ottoline, explaining,

> ❝ My future is as an uncharted sea, except where it is crossed by **Lytton's** system of soundings."

(Morgan has been reading a lot of Proust lately.)

Mid-May. **Virginia** writes to Ottoline canceling her Garsington visit for the last weekend in May. She's had three teeth pulled and can't shake off the flu. Maybe late June or early July?

Saturday, May 27. Forster is enjoying his weekend in Tidmarsh, chatting with **Lytton** and others. The surprise guests are **Virginia** and her husband **Leonard**, 41. Weren't they supposed to be at Garsington this weekend?

Ottoline sends a wire to Morgan and **Lytton** imploring them both to come to her garden party, about an hour away, which will go on all day. She wants them to visit with Tom Eliot. Carrying the **Woolfs'** secret with them, Morgan and **Lytton** set off.

At Garsington, the party is in full swing. Everyone is swimming in the pond and Ottoline is holding court, dressed in a picture hat and bright yellow satin top.

Forster always enjoys the gossip at these get-togethers but feels that a lot of the chatter when he's not in the room is about him.

🎋 MAY 2, 1922 🎋
TORONTO DAILY STAR, TORONTO

The article, "Getting a Hot Bath an Adventure in Genoa," appears in today's paper. The writer, the *Star's* European correspondent **Ernest Hemingway**, 22, covering the international Genoa Conference, reports that,

> 	❝ 	[UK Prime Minister] Lloyd George says that conferences are cheaper and better than war, but, as far as I know, Lloyd George has never been blown up by an exploding Italian bathroom. I just have been. This is one of the numerous differences between us..."

Toronto Daily Star, *May 2*

Hemingway goes on to describe his experience last month when, at the apartment where he was staying in Genoa, his bathroom water heater literally exploded and he was blown into a heavy wooden door. The hotel manager assured him that he was actually quite lucky—he was still alive, wasn't he? Alive, yes. Not seriously injured, yes. But definitely in pain.

However, **Ernie** didn't let this "adventure" keep him from his journalistic duties. He'd managed to get one of only 11 press passes to the hotel where the Russian delegation was staying—not a Bolshevik fan, **Hemingway** nevertheless admired how hard the Russians worked, late into the night—covered the Parisian Anti-Alcohol League—he found it well organized "while the consumers are not"—and filed detailed glowing descriptions of the British PM, chief organizer of the Conference of 34 nations.

Hemingway is back in Paris now. He is enjoying his stint as a journalist, but is more encouraged that the literary magazine, *The Double Dealer*, based in New Orleans, this month is publishing one of his stories, just two pages long, "A Divine Gesture." The editors claim they want to introduce those in the southern States to the new writing appearing elsewhere, but **Ernest** is the first new writer they have published so far this year.

❧ MAY 6, 1922 ❧
HOGARTH HOUSE, RICHMOND, LONDON

Facing serious dental work, including three extractions, and her inability to fight off this influenza that has had her in and out of bed for the past few months, the spring of novelist **Virginia Woolf's** 40th year is not going well.

Today, she and her husband **Leonard**, 41, were able to go for a walk. Hoorah! But then her temperature went up over 101 degrees, and they had to call the doctor.

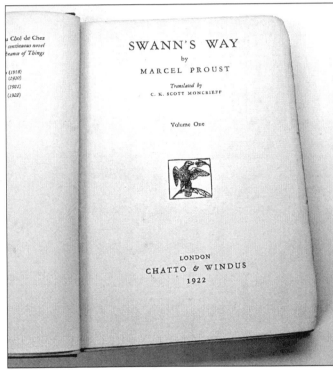

Swann's Way *by Marcel Proust*

The one bright spot is that, confined to bed, again, she now has time to delve back into the writing of Marcel Proust, 50.

She'd been introduced to his work during the Great War by her Bloomsbury friend, art critic **Roger Fry**, 55, whom she's writing to today. She tells **Roger** that, although she has the

> " most violent cold in the whole parish,...Proust's fat volume comes in very handy...to sink myself in it all day...Proust so titillates my own desire for expression that I can hardly set out the sentence. Oh if I could write like that! I cry. And at the moment such is the astonishing vibration and saturation and intensification that he procures—theres [sic] something sexual in it—that I feel I *can* write like that, and seize my pen and then I *can't* write like that. Scarcely anyone so stimulates the nerves of language in me: It becomes an obsession."

At the beginning of the year she had first taken up *Swann's Way*, and written to her fellow novelist E. M. Forster, 43, then in India,

> " Everyone is reading Proust. I sit silent and hear their reports. It seems to be a tremendous experience, but I'm shivering on the brink, and waiting to be submerged with a horrid sort of notion that I shall go down and down and down and perhaps never come up again."

Forster was so impressed by **Virginia's** reaction that he bought a copy of *Swann's Way* on board the ship back home to England. He has found that Proust's technique of revealing character through inner thoughts is influencing the India novel he is finally getting around to finishing.

Reading Proust is also helping **Woolf** with her work, a long short story, "Mrs. Dalloway in Bond Street." And it is keeping her from what she feels she is supposed to be reading, that vile tome, *Ulysses* by James Joyce, also 40.

❧ MID-MAY, 1922 ❧
HOTEL VENETIA, BOULEVARD MONTPARNASSE, PARIS

Having her Mom, Cora, 58, here for the past month or so has been a great distraction for American ex-pat poet Edna St. Vincent Millay, 30.

Cora and Edna are having a great time. Attending the Russian Ballet at the Opera House. Eating in the local cafes. Dancing at Zelli's, the Montmartre Club. Mom is a big hit.

Edna has moved them here from the original hotel she booked. As she explains in a letter to her sister,

66   because it [was] so cust expensive, and [we] are now in a cheap but not a very clean hotel…Two minutes from this bleeding kafe [the Rotonde] and just around the corner from the beautiful Luxembourg Gardens."

Since Cora's arrival, Edna has started seeing a Frenchman—whom Mom does not like. Not only does he borrow money, he shows up unexpectedly and takes Edna away from Cora. And he looks too much like her ex-husband.

Edna's love life has been on the skids so far this year.

Millay spent the first part of the year in Vienna, living with a former boyfriend, only because he could split expenses. She'd gone through her income from the poems and Nancy Boyd stories she is sending back to *Vanity Fair* and the $500 advance from Boni and Liveright for a raunchy novel she can't write.

One of her beaus, fellow poet Arthur Ficke, 38, back in America, asked her why she hadn't responded to the marriage proposal sent to her in a letter from Hal, writer Witter Bynner, 40, another of her conquests. She didn't even remember a marriage proposal?! Hal is good-looking, well-traveled, a Harvard grad, rich. She wrote to him to ask if he wants to get married, and when she didn't hear back right away she cabled him,

Yes!"

She even told her sister that she was "sort of engaged."

When Edna finally does get a letter from Hal, now living in Santa Fe, New Mexico, exhausted from a recent cross-country lecture tour, he explains that of course she must know the whole marriage thing was a joke.

Edna wrote back instantly,

 Oh, Lord—oh, Lord—Oh. *Hal!*"

Of course she knew it was a joke. Ha ha. The letters and cables she sent must have really frightened him. Thank God he hadn't taken her seriously! Ha ha.

Bastard.

Then came the crushing blow. Arthur writes to say that he is finally leaving his wife. For his girlfriend. Not Edna.

Millay is thinking she might as well try to marry the French guy.

❧ MAY 13, 1922 ❧
TORONTO DAILY STAR, TORONTO

Today, the last article about the International Genoa Conference by the *Star's* European correspondent, ex-pat American **Ernest Hemingway**, 21, appears in the paper. **Hemingway** writes a glowing profile of the UK Prime Minister and organizer of the conference, David Lloyd George, 59. He ends with the anecdote of an Italian boy presenting the PM with a portrait he had drawn of him, and Lloyd George being gracious enough to sign it:

> 66 I looked at the sketch. It wasn't bad. But it wasn't Lloyd George. The only thing that was alive in it was the sprawled-out signature, gallant, healthy, swashbuckling, careless and masterful, done in a moment and done for all time, it stood out among the dead lines of the sketch—it was Lloyd George."

❧ MAY 15, 1922 ❧
1729 MURRAY AVENUE, SQUIRREL HILL, PITTSBURGH, PENNSYLVANIA

In the Squirrel Hill neighborhood of Pittsburgh, Pennsylvania, the Manor Theatre opens with a showing of *Hail the Woman* starring Florence Vidor, 26, wife of noted film director King Vidor, 28. Piano accompaniment is included.

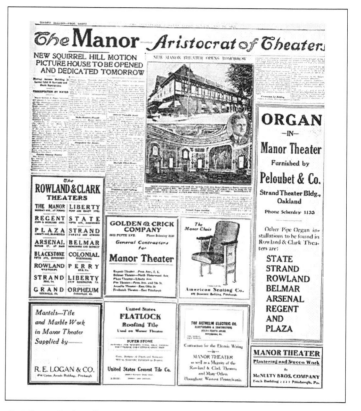

Article in the local newspaper announcing the opening of the Manor Theatre

❧ MAY 17, 1922 ❧
NEW YORK CITY, NEW YORK

American photographer Alfred Stieglitz, 58, has sent a questionnaire to other noted artists:

❝ Can a photograph have the significance of art?"

French painter Marcel Duchamp, 34, living in New York, replies:

❝ Dear Stieglitz,

Even a few words I don't feel like writing. You know exactly what I think of photography. I would like to see it make people despise painting until something else will make photography unbearable— There we are. Affectionately

Marcel Duchamp"

Marcel Duchamp *by Man Ray*

❧ MAY 18-19, 1922 ❧
MAJESTIC HOTEL, AVENUE KLEBER; AND
44 RUE DE L'AMIRAL-HAMELIN, PARIS

THE AFTER-THEATRE DINNER PARTY:

A Teleplay

SFX: *Renard* by Stravinsky

Long shot of the Paris Opera House. The camera moves in
to focus on the poster for tonight's performance:

Then a tight shot of the wording:

RENARD

Première mondiale! Musique
et livret d'Igor Stravinsky

Chorégraphie de Bronislava Nijinsky

Interprété par Les Ballets Russes,
sous la direction de Serge Diaghilev

Réalisé par Ernest Ansermet Avec des
décors conçus par Pablo Picasso

The camera pulls back and takes us through the streets
of the Right Bank to the entrance of the Hotel Majestic
on Avenue Kleber.

We follow the camera inside and up the stairs to a
private room. Stravinsky's music is drowned out by the

---

sounds of about 35 or 40 partygoers, formally dressed, chatting and laughing. Waiters are getting ready to serve dinner.

Speaking in front of the room is Russian impresario Serge Diaghilev, 50.

> DIAGHILEV: Thank you to our hosts for the evening, Mr. and Mrs. Sydney Schiff, who have brought together tonight the four living artists Mr. Schiff most admires [gesturing to each]: Monsieur Picasso, Monsieur Stravinsky, Monsieur Joyce [looks around the room] Monsieur Joyce? No? And Monsieur Proust [looks around the room again] Monsieur Proust?! No?

As he is speaking, the camera moves around the table to give close-ups of some of the dinner guests: Spanish painter Pablo Picasso, 40, with a Catalan sash tied around his head like a turban; his wife Olga, 30; French director Ernest Ansermet, 38; French composer Erik Satie, just turned 56; Russian composer Igor Stravinsky, 39; English patron Sydney Schiff, 53; his wife Violet, 48; and English art critic **Clive Bell**, 40.

> DIAGHILEV: I hope you all enjoy the dinner.

Waiters begin serving. Outside, bells chime midnight.

The camera moves around the room showing the partygoers enjoying the food and each other's company.

Fade to the same scene showing most of the food eaten and waiters slowly clearing a few plates and starting to serve coffee.

The camera settles on the door to the room and in staggers Irish author James Joyce, 40, looking confused, poorly dressed and a bit drunk. Sydney Schiff motions for a waiter to put a chair next to him, and Joyce sits in it. He puts his head in his hands, and a waiter sets a glass of champagne in front of him.

Panning back to the door, we see Marcel Proust, 50, enter, dressed in evening clothes and wearing white gloves. A chair is placed between Sydney Schiff and Stravinsky; Proust sits there. A waiter brings him some food and drink.

>PROUST, turning to Stravinsky: Monsieur Stravinsky, doubtless you admire Beethoven?

>STRAVINSKY, barely looking at him: I detest Beethoven.

>PROUST: But, *cher maitre*, surely those late sonatas and quartets...

>STRAVINSKY: Worse than all the others.

Ansermet, sitting nearby, leans over to talk to both of them to avoid having this discussion become a fight.

Snoring is heard, and the camera moves to focus on Joyce, who has nodded off.

Hearing the snoring, a posh woman seated next to **Clive Bell** tugs on his sleeve and whispers in his ear. The two get up, put on their coats and leave together. Sydney Schiff gets up to see them out.

As soon as they leave, Joyce wakes up and Proust leans over to talk to him:

>PROUST: Ah, Monsieur Joyce, you know the Princess...

>JOYCE: No, Monsieur.

PROUST: Ah. You know the Countess…

JOYCE: No, Monsieur.

PROUST: Then you know Madame…

JOYCE: No, Monsieur.

The camera moves away but we hear the two men still chatting.

People start pushing back their chairs, gathering their coats, getting ready to leave.

Proust turns to Sydney and Violet Schiff, asking if they would like to come to his apartment.

The three leave together, with Joyce following closely behind.

Outside the hotel, a car is waiting and all four wedge themselves in.

The camera follows the car just a few blocks to 44 rue de l'Amiral-Hamelin.

Joyce starts to get out of the car after the Schiffs and Proust, but Proust gestures for him to stay in and signals to the driver to continue on. Proust heads for his building while Sydney gives the driver specific instructions and then turns with his wife to follow Proust inside.

Inside the apartment we see Proust and the Schiffs happily chatting and drinking champagne as the camera pulls back to reveal the sun coming up outside the window.

FIN

❧ MAY 20-21, 1922 ❧
GORDON SQUARE, BLOOMSBURY; AND
HOGARTH HOUSE, RICHMOND, LONDON

In the Bloomsbury section of London, economist **John Maynard Keynes**, 39, is writing to his friend, painter **Vanessa Bell**, 42, about the living arrangements in Gordon Square for his current partner, Russian ballerina Lydia Lopokova, 30, and his former lover (and **Vanessa's** current partner) painter **Duncan Grant**, 37.

> If [Lydia] lived in 41, [**Duncan**] and I in 46, you and family in 50, and we all had meals in 46 that might not be a bad arrangement... We all want both to have and not have husbands and wives."

❧❧❧

Gordon Square

The next day, in Richmond, southwest London, **Vanessa's** sister, novelist **Virginia Woolf**, 40, is writing to a friend describing a conversation she and her husband **Leonard**, 41, had recently:

> **Leonard** says we owe a great deal to [George Bernard] Shaw. I say that he only influenced the outer fringe of morality...**Leonard** says rot; I say damn. Then we go home. **Leonard** says I'm narrow. I say he's stunted."

Now *that's* a marriage…

✣ LATE MAY, 1922 ✣
LOS ANGELES, CALIFORNIA

Where were they, he wonders? Where was his studio, Famous Players-Lasky? Where was his patron and supposed-supporter, producer Jesse Lasky, 41?

Rudolph Valentino, just turned 27, is their top movie star. He's already had two big hits released this year and what promises to be an even bigger smash, *Blood and Sand*, due out this summer.

But when he was thrown in prison a few days ago, on a felony charge of bigamy no less, Valentino had to raise bail from his friends; Lasky let him sit there and refused to come up with the cash.

Blood and Sand *poster*

Earlier this year, after his divorce was final, Valentino had announced his engagement to Natascha Rambova (really Winifred Shaughnessy Hudnut), 25, who had been the art director on one of his early films. This month they went to Mexicali, Mexico, and were legally married.

About a week after they returned to Los Angeles, a warrant was issued for Valentino's arrest! He and his lawyer went to the L. A.'s District Attorney's office so Rudolph could turn himself in and he was thrown in jail. Turns out California law requires both sides in a divorce to wait one year before re-marrying. Who knew?! Well, not Valentino or his lawyers apparently.

Rudolph has been told that there's a good chance these charges will be thrown out by the court because he hasn't even lived with his new wife yet.

Oh, great. Valentino knows that once that story gets into the papers, the public will think that he's homosexual.

❧ MAY 25, 1922 ❧
BROOK FARM, 845 NORTH SALEM ROAD, RIDGEFIELD, CONNECTICUT

Just a few days ago, Irish-American playwright Eugene O'Neill, 33, was awarded his second Pulitzer Prize for Drama, for *Anna Christie* which premiered last year. His first Pulitzer was for his first full-length play staged on Broadway, *Beyond the Horizon*, back in 1920. In addition to the awards, both plays received good reviews from the *New York Times* drama critic, **Alexander Woollcott**, 35, who told theatregoers that *Anna Christie* is "a singularly engrossing play…[that you] really ought to see." Other critics agreed.

His most recent, *The Hairy Ape*, started out with his Greenwich Village theatre troupe The Provincetown Players, but has just been transferred to the

Eugene O'Neill and his dog, Finn MacCool, which he kept at Brook Farm (right). Both pictures are from ca. 1923.—from "A Formidable Shadow" by D.C. Thomas

Eugene O'Neill with his dog and his farm

Plymouth Theater on Broadway. With the playwright's name in lights on the marquee, instead of any actors' names. Quite a tribute.

Although **Woollcott** likes *The Hairy Ape* as well, calling it "vital and interesting and teeming with life," the New York Police Department has deemed the play "obscene, indecent, impure." Because of its themes of working class rebellion, the mayor wants to shut it down to avoid labor riots. Really.

His success has enabled O'Neill and his wife, English writer Agnes Boulton, 28, and their son Shane, three, to move to this 31-acre Connecticut country house, with a library, a sun-room, four master bedrooms and servants' quarters. As well as an Irish wolfhound Eugene has named Finn MacCool.

He is also $40,000 in debt.

Today he is writing to a friend,

❝ Yes, I seem to be becoming the [Pulitzer] Prize Pup of Playwrights—the Hot Dog of the Drama. When the Police Department isn't pinning the Obscenity Medal on my *Hairy Ape* chest, why, then it's Columbia [University] adorning the brazen bosom of *Anna* with the Cross of Purity. I begin to feel that there is either something all wrong with me or something all right...'It's a mad world, my masters.'"

✺ MAY 28, 1922 ✺

SUNDAY EXPRESS, LONDON; AND
NEW YORK TIMES, NEW YORK CITY, NEW YORK

Two very different reviews of the new novel *Ulysses* by James Joyce, 40, appear on opposite sides of the pond today:

❝   I say deliberately that it is the most infamously obscene book in ancient or modern literature…All the secret sewers of vice are canalized in its flood of unimaginable thoughts, images and pornographic words. And its unclean lunacies are larded with appalling and revolting blasphemies directed against the Christian religion and against the name of Christ—blasphemies hitherto associated with the most degraded orgies of Satanism and the Black Mass…[*Ulysses*] is already the Bible of beings who are exiles and outcasts in this and every other civilized country…We must make our choice between the devil's disciples and the disciples of God, between Satanism and Christianity, between the sanctions of morality and the anarchy of art. The artists must be treated like any lesser criminal who tries to break the Christian code. For this is a battle that must be fought out to a clean finish: We cannot trust the soul of Europe to the guardianship of the police and the post office."

> —"Beauty and the Beast," James Douglas,
> editor, *London Sunday Express*

✺✺✺

❝   *Ulysses* is the most important contribution that has been made to fictional literature in the 20th century. It will immortalize its author with the same certainty that Gargantua and Pantagruel immortalized Rabelais, and *The Brothers Karamazof* [sic] Dostoyevsky. It is likely that no one writing English today could parallel Mr. Joyce's feat…His literary output would seem to substantiate some of Freud's contentions…He holds with Freud that the unconscious mind represents the real man…I have learned more psychology and psychiatry from it than I did in 10 years at the Neurological Institute. There are other angles at which *Ulysses* can be viewed profitably, but they are not many…[The protagonist Leopold Bloom is] a moral monster, a pervert and an invert, an apostate to his race and his religion, the simulacrum of a man who has neither cultural background nor personal self-respect…[*Ulysses* will be praised in 100 years, but] not 10 men or women out of a hundred can read *Ulysses* through."

—"James Joyce's Amazing Chronicle,"
Joseph Collins, *New York Times*

❧ JUNE 5, 1922 ❧
THOOR BALLYLEE, COUNTY GALWAY, IRELAND

The **Yeats** family is settling in nicely to their new home in the west of Ireland, a 15th century Norman tower they have re-named Thoor Ballylee.

The poet and playwright **William Butler Yeats**, about to turn 57, is impressed by the way his wife Georgie, 29, not only takes care of their two children, Anne, three, and Michael, almost 10 months old, but has also decorated their home to look like a 14th century painting.

Uncharacteristically, **Willie** has been thinking a lot about family. He has just sent off to his publisher the second volume of his *Autobiographies*, titled *The Trembling of the Veil*. His father, the painter John Butler Yeats, died about four months ago at age 82, in New York City. **Willie** and his sisters are thinking of bringing out a volume of their father's memoirs.

Coole Park

His friend and mentor, **Lady Augusta Gregory**, 70, has been at her home, Coole Park, about four miles down the road from Thoor Ballylee, working on her own memoirs about their days founding The Abbey Theatre together. She's been reading out sections to **Willie** and incorporating many of his suggestions. Their writing styles are very different—**Augusta** is trying to remain objective; **Yeats** favors a more impressionistic interpretation.

Now that *The Trembling of the Veil* is completed, today **Willie** is writing to his friend in New York, the Irish-American lawyer and patron of the arts, John Quinn, 51.

He brings Quinn up to date on the family living arrangements and tells him that his godson, Michael, now has eight teeth! Anne has invented her own version of "The Lord's Prayer," which includes, "Father not in heaven—father in the study," and "Thine is the Kitten, the Power, and the Glory."

Quinn had expressed his concern about how Ireland's political turmoil is impacting the west of the country. **Yeats** assures him that there hasn't been much trouble here:

 There was what seemed a raid at Coole, men came and shouted at night and demanded to be let in, and then went away either because the moon came out or because they only meant to threaten."

Most importantly, **Willie** wants his friend's permission to dedicate his latest volume to Quinn.

 If you violently object you must cable…for [Werner Laurie, the publisher] is in a devil of a hurry."

The dedication reads,

 To John Quinn my friend and helper and friend and helper of certain people mentioned in this book."

✵ JUNE 8, 1922 ✵
LIFE MAGAZINE, NEW YORK CITY, NEW YORK

The theatre critic for humor magazine *Life* had no trouble writing the review which appears today. The play *Abie's Irish Rose*, about a Jewish man in love with an Irish woman, just opened at the Fulton Theatre.

In "Drama: A Pair of Little Rascals," **Robert Benchley**, 32, makes it clear that he feels *Abie's* is "one of the season's worst," stating that

❝ *The Rotters* [which he also hated] is no longer the worst play in town!"

Bob is not alone. One of his lunch buddies from the Algonquin Hotel, **Heywood Broun**, 33, in the *New York World*, calls it,

❝ A synthetic farce…There is not so much as a single line of honest writing in it…No author has ever expressed her contempt for the audiences in such flagrant fashion as Miss Anne Nichols…[The play] seems designed to attract the attention of Irish and Jewish theatregoers but is likely to offend such patrons even a little more than any others…So cheap and offensive that it might serve to unite all the races in the world in a common hymn of hate."

Anne Nichols

One of their other lunch buddies, the dean of New York columnists, **FPA [Franklin Pierce Adams]**, 40, also in the *World*, deems it the worst play he has ever seen. And he's seen a lot.

But, true to form, another Algonquin lunch regular, **Alexander Woollcott**, 35, drama critic of the *New York Times*, loves it:

> ❝ *Abie's Irish Rose* is funny…A highly sophisticated Summer audience… [laughed] uproariously at [the play's] juggling with some fundamental things in human life, and at some others, not so fundamental, but deeply cherished, as lifelong feelings are wont to be."

Woollcott predicts it will run for years.

Benchley is more optimistic. He gives it a month. He dreads having to come up with a little capsule review of this turkey each week.

❧ JUNE, 1922 ❧

ON THE NEWSSTANDS OF AMERICA

The *Dial* magazine has "More Memories" by Irish playwright **William Butler Yeats**, just turned 57, and two line drawings by Spanish artist Pablo Picasso, 40. Its monthly columns include "Paris Letter" by American ex-pat poet Ezra Pound, 36, and "Dublin Letter" by the recently retired Head Librarian of the National Library of Ireland, John Eglinton, 54, actually writing from his home in Bournemouth, England. He reviews the new novel *Ulysses* by his fellow Dubliner, James Joyce, 40, living in Paris:

The Dial, *June*

66 I am by no means sure, however, that I have understood Mr. Joyce's method, which is sufficiently puzzling even where he relates incidents in which I have myself taken a humble part...There is an effort and a strain in the composition of this book which makes one feel at times a concern for the author. But why should we half-kill ourselves to write masterpieces? There is a growing divergence between the literary ideals of our artists and the books which human beings want to read."

The New York Times Book Review has a review of *The Secret Adversary*, the second novel from English writer Agatha Christie, 31:

The Secret Adversary *by Agatha Christie, U. S. edition*

    " Unless the reader peers into the last chapter or so of the tale, he will not know who this secret adversary is until the author chooses to reveal him…[Miss Christie] gives a sense of plausibility to the most preposterous situations and developments…[But she] has a clever prattling style that shifts easily into amusing dialogue and so aids the pleasure of the reader as he tears along with Tommy and Tuppence on the trail of the mysterious Mr. Brown. Many of the situations are a bit moth-eaten from frequent usage by other quarters, but at that Miss Christie manages to invest them with a new sense of individuality that renders them rather absorbing."

Metropolitan magazine has a piece, "Eulogy for the Flapper" by Zelda Fitzgerald, 22, who is considered to be the original flapper, as created in the two recent hit novels by her husband, **F. Scott Fitzgerald**, 25:

    " The flapper is deceased…They have won their case. They are blase… Flapperdom has become a game; it is no longer a philosophy."

The Smart Set has a short story by Zelda's husband, "The Diamond as Big as the Ritz":

    " [Percy Washington boasts that his father is] by far the richest man in the world and has a diamond bigger than the Ritz-Carlton Hotel."

The Saturday Evening Post has two pieces by friends who lunch together regularly at the midtown Manhattan Algonquin Hotel: "Men I'm Not Married To" by free-lance writer **Dorothy Parker**, 28, and "Women I'm Not Married To" by popular newspaper columnist **FPA [Franklin Pierce Adams]**, 40.

The Double Dealer, A National Magazine from the South, true to its mission to publish new work by new writers has "Portrait," a poem by recent University of Mississippi dropout, William Faulkner, 24, and "Ultimately," a four-line poem by *Toronto Star* foreign correspondent **Ernest Hemingway**, 22, a Chicago-an currently living in Paris:

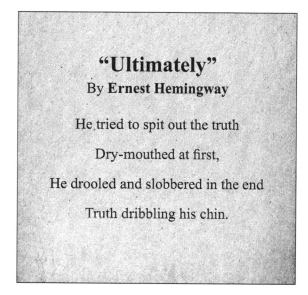

"Ultimately"
By Ernest Hemingway

He tried to spit out the truth

Dry-mouthed at first,

He drooled and slobbered in the end

Truth dribbling his chin.

❧ MID-JUNE, 1922 ❧
WYEWURK, 3 CRAIG STREET,
THIRROUL, NEW SOUTH WALES, AUSTRALIA;
AND THOMAS SELTZER, INC.,
5 WEST 50TH STREET, NEW YORK CITY, NEW YORK

When looking for a place to rent for their three-month stay in Australia, English writer David Herbert Lawrence, 36, and his German wife Frieda, 42, found this suburb to be less expensive—but definitely less glamorous—than nearby Sydney. They took this three-bedroom bungalow with a lovely veranda, on the beach outside Thirroul, even though they discovered the previous owner had named it "Wyewurk." Probably because the house next door was "Wyewurrie."

Lawrence has every intention of working. He started his new novel at the beginning of the month and is making great progress, sometimes as many as 3,000 words a day. With the title already decided, *Kangaroo* is turning out to be more autobiographical and more political than any of his others—and with a lot less sex.

Each day he sits at a big table looking out at the Pacific Ocean, turning the experiences he and Frieda have had since coming here, combined with political news he picks up from the *Sydney Bulletin*, into his eighth novel. David is incorporating the natural environment as well as the people they've met. Although he gives his two main characters quite a few more friends than he and Frieda actually have.

In the mornings while he is writing, Frieda is sewing and keeping house. In the afternoons, David reads out to her what he has written that day. Frieda writes to a friend,

❝ The days slipped by like dreams, but real as dreams are when they come true."

Of course, sometimes they fight. Or sulk. After all, it is just the two of them out in the middle of nowhere most of the time.

On afternoons like this one, with Frieda napping, David catches up on his correspondence. Earlier in the month he wrote to his American agent, Robert Mountsier, 34, to apprise him of his progress and request another $700 in U. S. royalties. He tells Mountsier he expects to leave Australia for America in early August with a completed manuscript in his luggage.

Now Lawrence is writing to his U. S. publisher, Thomas Seltzer, 47, to assure him that this novel won't have the same censorship problems of his previous ones, like *Women in Love*. He thinks Seltzer, as a founder and former editor of the Socialist magazine *The Masses*, will appreciate the political nature of *Kangaroo*. He promises,

> ❝ No love interest at all so far—don't intend any—no sex either…Amy Lowell says you are getting a reputation as an erotic publisher: She warns me. I shall have thought my reputation as an erotic writer (poor dears) was secure. So now I'll go back on it."

Of course, he has promised Seltzer this before.

⚜

In his office across from St. Patrick's Cathedral, Seltzer is writing to Lawrence's agent, Mountsier, who is on vacation in Pennsylvania. The agent has been complaining about Lawrence's slow sales, and Seltzer has just paid for some advertising in the *New York Tribune* for Lawrence's latest, *Aaron's Rod*:

Logo of Thomas Seltzer, Inc.

> ❝ The work of a great genius and a bestseller. Love and Marriage in our day as Lawrence sees it."

To impress the agent even more with their author's reputation, he cites a new revue, *The Grand Street Follies*, currently playing in lower Manhattan at the Neighborhood Playhouse. In one scene, a young woman ignores her boyfriend while she is reading a book, saying,

" Don't interrupt me…I am in the midst of one of the most passionate passages of D. H. Lawrence."

Seltzer assures Mountsier,

" This, they say, always brings the house down."

❧ JUNE **19, 1922** ❧
GORDON SQUARE, BLOOMSBURY, LONDON

The party seems to be going well.

Art critic **Clive Bell**, 40, is hosting the dinner party following this evening's meeting of The Memoir Club.

The Club was started a couple of years ago by about a dozen friends, family and lovers who live in and around the Bloomsbury section of London. Kept totally private, the main purpose of the organization is to get its members thinking about writing their own autobiographies. And because those who read out papers at the get-togethers are bound by the rules to be as candid as possible, The Memoir Club provides delightful entertainment as well.

Tonight's presenters include **Lytton Strachey**, 42, whose biography of *Queen Victoria* was a big hit last year, and novelist Edward Morgan Forster, 43, recently returned from another trip to India.

Forster is in particularly good form tonight. By happy accident he has become the main topic of conversation in the letters page of the *London Times*.

At the beginning of the month, the *Times'* review of *Da Silva's Widow and Other Stories* by "Lucas Malet"—in reality Mary St. Leger Kinsley, 70—compared the book to Forster's 1911 collection of six short stories, *The Celestial Omnibus*. Truth be told, Forster's stories hadn't sold well.

But the mention in the *Times* set off a volley of letters of praise for Forster's writing, almost every day for two weeks, headlined "Mr. E. M. Forster's Books." This culminated in a letter from Kingsley herself who claimed she had never heard of him.

Well. She sure has heard of him now. The publisher of *Celestial Omnibus* wrote in offering a free copy of Forster's book to anyone who made the same claim. A previous publisher got in touch, inquiring if Morgan was working on another novel. And sales soared.

Reveling in his newfound fame, Morgan is feeling confident sharing pieces of his memoir and chatting with his Bloomsbury friends.

At the dinner, most of the discussion however is about a new long poem by another friend of theirs, the American ex-patriate Thomas Stearns Eliot, 33, which he calls "The Waste Land." Eliot has been reading it out to friends over the past few months, and writer Mary Hutchinson, 33, **Clive's** current mistress, calls it "Tom's autobiography—a melancholy one."

Clive's sister-in-law, novelist **Virginia Woolf**, 40, agrees with Mary's opinion of the poem, but **Virginia** has been jealous of Hutchinson in the past. Tonight Mary is being quite kind. **Virginia** records in her diary later that Mary "crossed the room & purred in my ear."

❧ JUNE 21, 1922 ❧
31 NASSAU STREET, NEW YORK CITY, NEW YORK

About three years ago, New York lawyer John Quinn, 51, had helped to negotiate a contract for American poet living in London T. S. Eliot, then 30, with Alfred A. Knopf, Inc. for the publication of his *Poems*. Eliot had felt that the original contract advantaged the publisher more than the published. Quinn was glad to do it; he advised Eliot that he was well-known enough now to secure the services of a literary agent and hadn't heard from him since.

Through their mutual friend, another American poet living abroad, Ezra Pound, 36, Quinn knows that

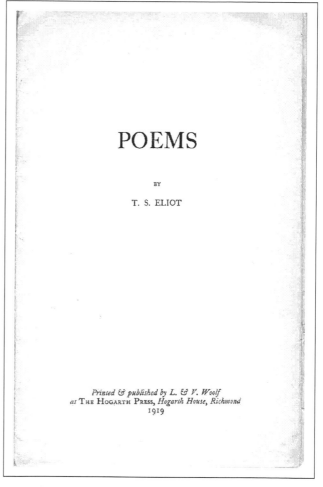

POEMS

BY

T. S. ELIOT

*Printed & published by L. & V. Woolf
at* THE HOGARTH PRESS, *Hogarth House, Richmond*
1919

Poems *by T. S. Eliot, UK edition*

Eliot is working on a "big" poem, probably his best work.

Today, Quinn receives a telegram from Eliot in London:

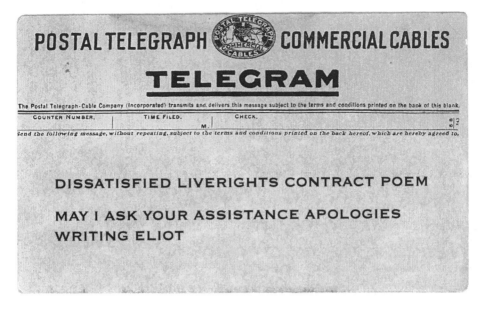

Quinn cables back right away:

The second cable he sends today is to his Irish friend, poet and playwright
William Butler Yeats, just turned 57, who has written to ask if he may
dedicate his memoirs to Quinn:

POSTAL TELEGRAPH COMMERCIAL CABLES

TELEGRAM

The Postal Telegraph-Cable Company (Incorporated) transmits and delivers this message subject to the terms and conditions printed on the back of this blank.

| COUNTER NUMBER. | TIME FILED. | CHECK. |

Send the following message, without repeating, subject to the terms and conditions printed on the back hereof, which are hereby agreed to.

YEATS
BALLYLEE
GORT
COUNTY GALWAY
IRELAND

GREATLY TOUCHED AND DELIGHTED YOUR
SUGGESTION DEDICATION MEMOIRS.

GLADLY ACCEPT THO PERSONALLY FEEL
LADY GREGORY DESERVES THAT HONOR
MUCH MORE THAN I.

(SIGNED) QUINN

❧ JUNE 24, 1922 ❧
TORONTO DAILY STAR AND
TORONTO STAR WEEKLY, TORONTO

The newspaper's foreign correspondent, **Ernest Hemingway**, 22, former Chicago-an now living in Paris, has been getting his bylined pieces in the paper fairly regularly. Today there are two—his interview with the head of Italy's National Fascist Party, Benito Mussolini, 38, in the *Daily Star*, and a more in-depth "think" piece about the impact of the strongman's actions in the *Star Weekly*.

Getting the interview involved more luck than planning. **Hemingway** was in Milan for a belated second honeymoon with his wife, Hadley, 30, so he could show her where he had served in the Red Cross ambulance corps during the Great War.

When **Ernest** heard that Mussolini was in town, he whipped out his press credentials and blagged his way into the offices of *Popolo d'Italia*, the newspaper which Mussolini founded eight years ago and still edits.

Hemingway was impressed with his fellow journalist/war veteran's strength. In "Fascisti Party Half-Million," he leads his profile with a description,

> Benito Mussolini, head of the Fascisti movement, sits at his desk at the fuse of the great powder magazine that he has laid through all Northern and Central Italy and occasionally fondles the ears of a wolfhound pup, looking like a short-eared jack rabbit, that plays with the papers on the floor beside the big desk. Mussolini is a big, brown-faced man with a high forehead, a slow smiling mouth, and large, expressive hands...Mussolini was a great surprise. He is not the monster he has been pictured. His face is intellectual, it is the typical 'Bersagliere' [Italian Army infantry] face, with its large, brown, oval shape, dark eyes and big, slow speaking mouth."

In his complementary commentary in the *Star Weekly*, **Ernest** focuses more on the dangers of the Fascisti's rise. He points out that the Blackshirt movement "had a taste for killing under police protection and they liked it." The lira is tanking; the Communists have formed an opposition movement called the Redshirts; and many Italian mafioso are rushing to emigrate to the States.

Hemingway concludes his piece:

❝ ❝ The whole business has the quiet and peaceful look of a three-year-old child playing with a live Mills bomb."

You can read more of Hemingway's Mussolini profile here. https://thegrandarchive.wordpress. com/fascisti-party-now-ten-million-strong/

❧ JUNE 28, 1922 ❧
FOUR COURTS, DUBLIN; AND
THOOR BALLYLEE, COUNTY GALWAY, IRELAND;
MUNICH AND BERLIN, GERMANY

In the general election almost two weeks ago, candidates supporting the Treaty recently negotiated with Britain won more seats in the Dail than those against. The sore losers, led by Eamon de Valera, 39, seized the Four Courts in Dublin.

Under pressure from the impatient British government, Michael Collins, 31, leader of the pro-Treaty side and now Commander-in-Chief of the National Army, drove them out today. The Battle for Dublin and the larger Irish Civil War has begun.

Eamon de Valera

❧❧

In his castle in the west of Ireland, **William Butler Yeats**, 57, poet and co-founder of the Abbey Theater, writes to a friend,

66   All is I think going well and the principal result of all this turmoil will be love of order in the people and a stability in the government not otherwise obtainable…"

❧❧

Four days ago in Munich, the rabble-rousing Adolph Hitler, 33, leader of the National Socialist German Workers Party, entered the Stadelheim prison to begin serving his 100-day sentence for assaulting a political rival to keep him from giving a public speech.

⁂

Four days ago in Berlin, far-right terrorists assassinated liberal Jewish industrialist and politician Walther Rathenau, 54.

Friends inform last year's Nobel Laureate in Physics, Albert Einstein, 43, that he is on the same terrorists' hit list as Rathenau.

Albert decides that this would be a good time to embark on the numerous international trips he has been planning.

Thanks once again to Neil Weatherall, author of the play The Passion of the Playboy Riots, *for his help in sorting out Irish history.*

❧ JULY 1, 1922 ❧
SHILLINGSTONE, NORTH DORSET, ENGLAND

Cora Millay, 59, knows that she has to write to her family back in the States to explain why she and her daughter, poet Edna St. Vincent Millay, 30, have so suddenly moved from Paris to this little southern England village.

As a trained nurse, Cora is concerned about Vincent's health, she tells them. Stomach pain, "a bad time" with her bowels due to all that rich French food. And Millay

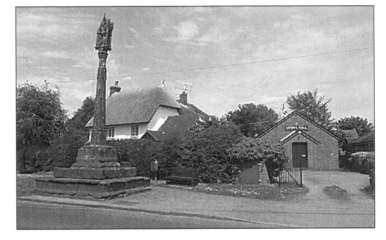

Shillingstone, Dorset

is exhausted by having to turn out regular articles for *Vanity Fair* magazine, as their foreign correspondent. Cora feels she will be much better here than back in noisy Paris, she writes.

As a trained nurse, Cora knows morning sickness when she sees it. Before they left, she wrote a nasty letter to the no-good Frenchman Vincent had been sleeping with, threatening him if he didn't leave her daughter alone. Cora calls him a "snake-headed fish." Vincent can't remember his name anymore.

Now that they are housed in this quiet cottage, with a garden and a piano, Cora has been taking Vincent on 12-mile hikes hoping for a miscarriage. She is feeding her a steady diet of folk remedies she is sure will work: clover, milk thistle, nettles, pigweed, henbane, gentian and borage. Fingers crossed.

❦ JULY, 1922 ❧
DUBLIN; NEW YORK CITY, NEW YORK; AND
74 GLOUCESTER PLACE, MARYLEBONE, LONDON

"The Confessions of James Joyce," by Mary Colum, 38, appears in Dublin's *Freeman's Journal*, the employer of *Ulysses* protagonist Leopold Bloom:

❝ The author himself takes no pains at all to make it easy of comprehension…What actually has James Joyce achieved in this monumental work? He has achieved what comes pretty near to being a satire on all literature. He has written down a page of his country's history. He has given the minds of a couple of men with a kind of actuality not hitherto found in literature. He has given us an impression of his own life and mind such as no other writer has given us before; not even Rousseau, whom he resembles."

"*Ulysses*" by Edmund Wilson, 27, appears in *The New Republic*:

❝ [Joyce] cannot be a realistic novelist…and write burlesques at the same time…[These 700 pages] are probably the most completely 'written' pages to be seen in any novel since Flaubert…[Joyce uses dialects] to record all the eddies and stagnancies of thought…[Despite its flaws it is] high genius…*Ulysses* has the effect at once of making everything else look brassy. Since I have read it, the texture of other novelists seems intolerably loose and careless; when I come suddenly unawares upon a page I have written myself I quake like a guilty thing surprised…If he repeats Flaubert's vices—as not a few have done—he also repeats his triumphs—which almost nobody has done…If he has really laid down his pen never to take it up again [as is rumored] he must know that the hand which laid it down upon the great affirmative of Mrs. Bloom, though it never writes another word, is already the hand of a master."

Advertising copywriter and would-be poet Hart Crane, 22, writes to a friend:

❝   I feel like shouting EUREKA!

You will pardon my strength of opinion on the thing, but [*Ulysses*] appears to me easily the epic of the age. It is as great a thing as Goethe's *Faust* to which it has a distinct resemblance in many ways. The sharp beauty and sensitivity of the thing! The matchless details!...

It is my opinion that some fanatic will kill Joyce sometime soon for the wonderful things said in *Ulysses*…"

❧❀❧

In London, one of Joyce's many benefactors, Harriet Shaw Weaver, 45, has decided that she will use her Egoist Press to publish *Ulysses* in the UK. Her lawyer warns her that producing a "private edition" will show the judges that she is restricting who can read it but won't have any other legal advantage. Her printer, Pelican Press, looks over the first 10 chapters and agrees to produce the book. But then someone there reads the rest of the novel and changes their decision.

Harriet figures she can have it printed, bound and packaged in Paris, where no one cares if it's "obscene," and

Harriet Shaw Weaver

then shipped over to England. She intends to correct all the typographical errors that are strewn throughout the first, hasty, printing, and sell direct to the public instead of through bookstores, to reduce the chances of confiscation. And she'll give Joyce 90% of the profit after expenses.

✣ JULY 7, 1922 ✣

THOMAS SELTZER, INC., 5 WEST 50TH STREET, NEW YORK CITY, NEW YORK

Late on this hot Friday afternoon, Thomas Seltzer, 47, is working at his desk in the office of his publishing company.

Suddenly, there is noise outside the door and in walks John Sumner, 45, head of the New York Society for the Suppression of Vice (NYSSV). Accompanying him is an officer of the West Side Police Court with a search warrant. They seize almost 800 copies—and also books from other publishers stored in Seltzer's own locked desk—of three books: the novella *Casanova's Homecoming* by the Austrian author Arthur Schnitzler, 60; *A Young Girl's Diary*, by an anonymous author, with a foreword by noted psychoanalyst Sigmund Freud, 66: and *Women in Love*, a novel by one of Seltzer's star authors, Englishman D. H. Lawrence, 36. Lawrence's most recent best seller, *Aaron's Rod*, is there in plain sight, but Sumner ignores it.

Unfortunately, there are lots of copies of *Women in Love* in the office because Lawrence's novel has not done as well as Seltzer expected.

Sumner informs the publisher that he is being charged under the New York State Penal Code for "the publication and sale of obscene literature." Sumner says he will have a police patrol car come by and haul away the books. Seltzer decides he will rent a truck to take them to the police station so the books themselves will not appear to be criminals under arrest.

Sumner is Executive Secretary of the NYSSV, which is empowered by the city to search and seize any materials the Society deems obscene. But Sumner is just a private citizen, so he issues Seltzer a receipt for the books in the name of the New York District Attorney.

The NYSSV also confiscates copies of the *Young Girl's Diary* from Brentano's bookstore and arrests a clerk at a local circulating library for lending out that book to "diverse persons."

Seltzer knows that he will need to consult his attorney before he takes any action, but his instinct is to fight these charges and to fight them quite publicly. This is going to be a big financial blow to his three-year-old publishing company, but his wife Adele, 46, a partner in his business, will support his decision. She is an even bigger fan of Lawrence than Seltzer is.

❧ EARLY JULY, 1922 ❧
CAP D'ANTIBES, COTE D'AZUR, FRANCE

American ex-pat Sara Wiborg Murphy, 38, heiress to the Wiborg ink company fortune, is sitting in a cove on La Garoupe beach, keeping an eye on her three children—Honoria, four; Baoth, three; Patrick, 18 months— and her husband, Gerald, 34, heir to the Mark Cross company fortune. Lounging on a tan rug under a sun umbrella, Sara's swimsuit straps are off her shoulders and her long string of pearls is draped down her back.

Cole Porter

Gerald, in a cap and stripey swimsuit, and their host, American composer Cole Porter, just turned 31, are raking seaweed and stones, about three feet thick, to make the sand a bit more pleasant.

Cole is mostly known for writing the scores to the *Hitchy-Koo* Broadway revues and Gerald is studying painting in Paris.

When the Murphys first decided to take a holiday at the beginning of this month, during their first summer living in Paris, they chose Houlgate, a resort in Normandy on the English Channel.

Horrible. Even having some friends staying close by wasn't enough to make up for the crap weather.

Back in Paris, Cole, and his wealthy wife Linda, 38, convinced them to come south with them to the Riviera for the next few weeks. They've rented a chateau because none of the hotels stay open past the end of the season in May. The locals think, what kind of people would want to come here in the hot summer?! And sit in the sun?! Apparently Americans do. And some Brits.

The Murphys and the Porters are loving it.

The Murphys at Houlgate

They nosh on some light refreshments—sherry, crackers—and will soon head back to the chateau for lunch.

Gerald and Sara have already decided—they will definitely come back here next summer.

❧ JULY, 1922 ❧
INDEPENDENT GALLERY, 7A GRAFTON STREET, MAYFAIR, LONDON

The one-person show at the Independent Gallery is going well. Painter **Vanessa Bell**, 43, has wanted to have her own show for many years now. She was jealous when her partner, painter **Duncan Grant**, 37, had his first solo exhibit about two years ago. Last winter, when they were in St. Tropez together, she produced several still lifes and interiors which are included here.

There are works by a former member of the Fauve movement, French painter Orthon Friesz, 43, in the next room. But she's got this one all to herself.

The day after the show opened in May, she wrote to her husband, art critic **Clive Bell**, 40:

❝ I am astonished that I have already sold seven pictures and drawings—so at any rate I shan't be out of pocket over it—[Gallery owner Percy Moore] Turner is very much pleased."

Last month, her Bloomsbury friend, **Roger Fry**, 55, gave her a glowing write up in *New Statesman.* He felt the portrait *Woman in Furs*, which **Vanessa** painted three years ago at her East Sussex home, Charleston Farmhouse, is "perhaps the most brilliant thing in the exhibit."

But this month she received an even more significant review in *The Burlington Magazine* from the influential painter Walter Sickert, 62:

❝ Instinct and intelligence and a certain scholarly tact have made her a good painter. The medium bends beneath her like a horse that knows its rider. In the canvas *The Frozen Pond*…the full resources of the medium in all its beauty have been called in to requisition in a manner which is nothing less than masterly."

Percy Moore Turner

Sickert has praised her work before. But this feels even more satisfying than **Roger's** compliments.

After all, she never slept with Sickert.

❧ SUMMER, 1922 ❧

MANHATTAN, NEW YORK CITY, NEW YORK

So far it's been one helluva summer for free-lance writer **Dorothy Parker**, soon to turn 29.

She and her husband of five years, Edwin Pond Parker II, 29, spent Memorial Day in Connecticut with his family. Eddie is thinking that they should move there. **Dottie** tried to get some writing done that weekend, but…no.

Then, soon after the Fourth of July, she comes home to find Eddie all packed up and ready to move out. He says he is fed up with his job at Paine Webber and he's moving back to Hartford with his family. She can have the dog and the furniture. Well, of course she'll keep the dog.

Dorothy tells her fellow writers who she lunches with regularly at the Algonquin Hotel that the split is amicable. It's just because Eddie took a new job in Hartford. They don't believe that for a minute.

A gossip columnist had recently implied that **Dorothy** and one of her lunch buddies, theatre critic **Robert Benchley**, 32, were having an affair because they are seen together around town all the time. **Dottie** and **Bob** reassured Eddie that it was just because their jobs are so similar. They review the same plays, are invited to the same parties, go to the same speakeasies, and have lunch together almost every day. That's all.

Despite the turmoil in her personal life. **Parker's** writing is going well. She had a piece in the *Saturday Evening Post* recently, "Men I'm Not Married To," as a companion to "Women I'm Not Married To" by her Algonquin friend **Franklin Pierce Adams [FPA]**, 40, in the same issue. There has been some talk of publishing the two together as a book. The *Post* runs something of hers in almost every issue.

Parker has also decided to expand beyond the little nonsense verses she's known for to try her hand at short stories. **FPA** is encouraging her; he gave her a book of French poetry and suggested that she can work on her prose style by

"Men I'm Not Married To," Saturday Evening Post

modeling these poems. **Parker** has also learned that she can't write fiction on a typewriter; she has switched to longhand, revising as she goes along.

Her first story is about a man clipping the hedges at his home in Scarsdale, ruminating about how trapped he feels by his wife, his kids, his mortgage, the suburbs. Something like **Benchley**. A bit depressing compared to her usual work, but *The Smart Set* has offered her $50 to publish it later in the year.

And just as she feels she is getting her life straightened out, along comes would-be playwright Charles MacArthur, 26. Fresh into Manhattan from Chicago; six feet tall; curly brown hair; with a line many women can die for. And fall for. Including **Dottie**.

They were introduced by her other lunch buddy, theatre critic **Alexander Woollcott**, 35, who likes MacArthur so much you'd think *he* was in love with him.

❝   What a perfect world this would be if it were full of MacArthurs!"

he has said.

Apparently, Charlie has a wife back in Chicago. No mind. **Dorothy** has a husband in Hartford. MacArthur bitches about the phoniness of New York City all the time, but knows he has to live here if he's going to have any kind of theatre career. One day he showed up at the ASPCA pound with birthday cakes for all the puppies. They both like scotch and they both like sex. How could **Dottie** not fall in love with him?!

Her Algonquin friends think it's cute, but surely **Dorothy** knows his reputation. He's been sleeping with so many women around town, magazine illustrator Neysa McMein, 34, has a rubber stamp made for him that says

❦ LATE JULY, 1922 ❧
WEST EGG, LONG ISLAND;
MANHATTAN, NEW YORK CITY, NEW YORK; AND
626 GOODRICH AVENUE, ST. PAUL, MINNESOTA

Midwestern bond salesman Nick Carraway, 30, is spending the summer working in Manhattan and living in a rented bungalow out on Long Island. Slowly, he is getting to know his neighbors:

At 9 o'clock one morning late in July, [Jay] Gatsby's gorgeous car lurched up the rocky drive to my door and gave out a burst of melody from its three-noted horn. It was the first time he had called on me, though I had gone to two of his parties, mounted in his hydroplane, and, at his urgent invitation, made frequent use of his beach.

'Good morning, old sport. You're having lunch with me today and I thought we'd ride up together.'

…He was never quite still; there was always a tapping foot somewhere or the impatient opening and closing of a hand.

He saw me looking with admiration at his car.

'It's pretty, isn't it, old sport?' He jumped off to give me a better view. 'Haven't you ever seen it before?'

I'd seen it. Everybody had seen it."

❧❦

Gatsby and Carraway have an interesting lunch in the city with one of Gatsby's friends, which ends when the friend gets up to leave:

'I have enjoyed my lunch,' he said, 'and I'm going to run off from you two young men before I outstay my welcome.'

'Don't hurry, Meyer,' said Gatsby without enthusiasm. Mr. Wolfsheim raised his hand in a sort of benediction.

'You're very polite, but I belong to another generation,' he announced solemnly. 'You sit here and discuss your sports and your young ladies and your—' He supplied an imaginary noun with another wave of his hand. 'As for me, I am 50 years old, and I won't impose myself on you any longer.'

As he shook hands and turned away his tragic nose was trembling. I wondered if I had said anything to offend him.

'He becomes very sentimental sometimes,' explained Gatsby. 'This is one of his sentimental days. He's quite a character around New York—a denizen of Broadway.'

'Who is he, anyhow, an actor?'

'No.'

'A dentist?'

'Meyer Wolfsheim? No, he's a gambler.' Gatsby hesitated, then added coolly: 'He's the man who fixed the World Series back in 1919.'

'Fixed the World Series?' I repeated.

The idea staggered me. I remembered, of course, that the World Series had been fixed in 1919, but if I had thought of it at all I would have thought of it as a thing that merely *happened*, the end of some inevitable chain. It never occurred to me that one man could start to play with the faith of 50 million people—with the single-mindedness of a burglar blowing up a safe.

'How did he happen to do that?' I asked after a minute.

'He just saw the opportunity.'

'Why isn't he in jail?'

'They can't get him, old sport. He's a smart man.'"

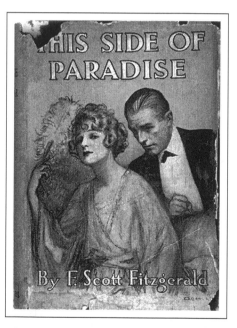

Back home in St. Paul, where he has started work on his third novel, best-selling writer **F. Scott Fitzgerald**, 25, has received an interesting offer.

A leading Hollywood producer is interested in buying the rights to **Fitzgerald's** first novel, *This Side of Paradise*, published two years ago. And he has suggested that the lead characters could be played on screen by **Scott** and his wife, Zelda, just turned 22.

Scott is considering it. Even though he tells his editor at Scribner's, Maxwell Perkins, 37, that this would be their "first and last appearance positively," Max knows the **Fitzgeralds** better than that. He manages to talk **Scott** out of it.

This Side of Paradise

❧ JULY 22, 1922 ❧

TORONTO DAILY STAR, TORONTO; AND *SATURDAY EVENING POST* MAGAZINE, NEW YORK CITY, NEW YORK

A Veteran Visits the Old Front" by the paper's foreign correspondent, American **Ernest Hemingway**, just turned 23, appears today in the *Toronto Daily Star*:

> PARIS.—Don't go back to visit the old front. If you have pictures in your head of something that happened in the night in the mud at Paschendaele or of the first wave working up the slope of Vimy, do not try and go back to verify them. It is no good...
>
> Go to someone else's front, if you want to. There your imagination will help you out and you may be able to picture the things that happened...I know because I have just been back to my own front...
>
> I have just come from Schio,...the finest town I remember in the war, and I wouldn't have recognized it now—and I would give a lot not to have gone...
>
> All the kick had gone out of things. Early next morning I left in the rain after a bad night's sleep...
>
> I tried to find some trace of the old trenches to show my wife, but there was only the smooth green slope. In a thick prickly patch of hedge we found an old rusty piece of shell fragment...That was all there was left of the front.
>
> For a reconstructed town is much sadder than a devastated town. The people haven't their homes back. They have new homes. The home they played in as children, the room where they made love with the lamp turned down, the hearth where they sat, the church they were married in, the room where their child died, these rooms are gone...

Now there is just the new, ugly futility of it all. Everything is just as it was—except a little worse...

I had tried to re-create something for my wife and had failed utterly. The past was as dead as a busted Victrola record. Chasing yesterdays is a bum show—and if you have to prove it, go back to your old front."

❧❦❧

This same day, "Welcome Home" by New York free-lance writer **Dorothy Parker**, 28, appears in the *Saturday Evening Post*:

❝ If at any time you happened to be hunting around for an average New York couple you couldn't make a better selection than my friends [Mr. and Mrs. Joseph Watson Lunt]...

Once a year, however, the Lunts lay aside the cloistered life, and burn up Broadway. This is on the occasion of the annual metropolitan visit of Mr. Lunt's Aunt Caroline, from the town where he spent his boyhood days...

The moment she sets foot in the Grand Central Terminal she compares it audibly and unfavorably with the new railroad station back home, built as soon as a decent interval had elapsed after the old one burned to the ground...

In the short ride to the Lunt apartment she manages to work in at least three times the line about 'New York may be all right for a visit, but I wouldn't live here if you gave me the place.'...

Once a year, when advertising in America can manage to stagger along without Mr. Lunt for three or four days, the Lunts do their share in the way of tightening up the home ties by paying a visit to Aunt Caroline...She meets them at the train, beaming with welcome and bubbling with exclamations of how glad they must be to get out of that horrid old New York...

And so the time goes by, till the Lunts must return to New York. Aunt Caroline is annually pretty badly broken up over their leaving for that awful city…

The only thing that keeps her from going completely to pieces is the thought that she has again brought into their sultry lives a breath of real life.

The Lunts blow the annual kisses to her from the parlor-car window… As Mr. Lunt sums it up, it's all right for a visit, but he wouldn't live there if you gave him the place."

You can read the full Hemingway article here, file:///C:/Users/Kathleen%20Donnelly/Desktop/ KD'S%20STUFF/such%20friends%20good/PARIS/Hemingway_Old_Front.pdf

And the full Parker essay here. https://babel.hathitrust.org/cgi/pt?id=uiug.30112041727428& view=1up&seq=283&skin=2021&q1=dorothy%20parker

🎐 LATE JULY, 1922 🎐
VILLA BEAUREGARD, GRAND RUE, DINARD, FRANCE

S itting on the beach, looking over the water to St. Malo, Spanish painter
Pablo Picasso, 40, is thankful that there has been a break in the rain.

Pablo and his family—his
wife, Russian-Ukrainian
ballerina Olga, 31, and their
almost 18-month old son,
Paolo, who is teething—came
to Brittany from Paris a
couple of weeks ago. Pablo
would have preferred spending
the summer in sunny Midi,
but Olga wanted Brittany.
After about a week, they
moved out of the hotel to this
villa on the beach.

When the weather is nice,
Pablo paints outdoors; he
has finished a few paintings
and quite a lot of drawings of
people on the beach.

But it has been mostly raining,
so the tourists crowd the two
casinos and the town's hotel

Olga Picasso

ballrooms. Inside their rented home, Pablo does sketches of Olga and Paolo
as well as the exterior and interiors of the villa. Despite his wife's whining
about her "woman problems," an endless stream of visiting friends, and his
screaming son, Pablo has managed to produce a surprising amount of work.

The baby screaming he can understand; but the wife is just plain annoying.

❧ JULY 30, 1922 ❧

CENTRAL PARK WEST, NEW YORK CITY, NEW YORK

If Irish-American lawyer and patron of the arts John Quinn, 52, wants to get out of the city as planned to spend all of August with his sister and niece in the Adirondacks, he has a bit of correspondence to catch up on.

Quinn has been corresponding with his emissary in Paris, Henri-Pierre Roche, 43, about leaving his best French paintings to the government of France, to be cared for in the Louvre. Roche has been negotiating to have Quinn acquire *The Circus* by Seurat. Roche wrote to him at the beginning of the month about a crazy day when he and Spanish painter Pablo Picasso, 40, went flying around Paris carrying a Cezanne landscape with them in a taxi, stopping at every shop to buy up all the suitable frames they could find.

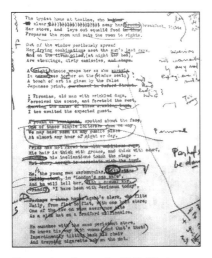

Typescript of poem by T. S. Eliot

One of the writers Quinn supports, American T. S. Eliot, 33, living in London, has written to give him power of attorney when negotiating a contract with Boni and Liveright to publish his latest work, an untitled lengthy poem. They are not sure, however, if it will be lengthy enough to appear as a book. Eliot writes that he is planning to add some notes to make it fatter. Quinn is finally getting around to reading the typescript Eliot has sent and is turning it over to his office secretary to make a copy that can be submitted to Liveright.

Quinn is finishing off a lengthy letter to one of his Irish friends, poet and painter **AE** (**George Russell**, 55). Their mutual friend, **Lady Augusta Gregory**, 70, had recently asked Quinn to recommend painters for inclusion in the Hugh Lane Gallery, which she is trying to establish in memory of her nephew who went down with the

Lusitania seven years ago. Quinn reports to **AE** that he told her that of the dead ones he would rank, in order, Cezanne, Seurat (much better than Renoir), and Rousseau. He puts Gauguin and van Gogh a bit farther down.

Of living artists he would include Picasso, Georges Braque, 40; Andre Derain, 42; and Henri Matisse, 52; in the first tier. In the second, Raoul Dufy, 45; Constantin Brancusi, 46—whom he has become good friends with—and Georges Rouault, 51.

Quinn tells **AE** that he would add a third tier of the living: Juan Gris, 35; Marie Laurencin, 39; and Jacques Villon, about to turn 47, among others.

Quinn's longest letter is to another Irish friend, poet and playwright, **William Butler Yeats**, 57. He brings **Willie** up to date on the recent funeral of his father, whom Quinn had taken care of during the past 15 years in New York City. The **Yeats** family decided it would be better for Dad to be buried in the States, and Quinn arranged a site in upstate New York:

> ““ If you and your sisters could see the place, I am sure you would have approved of [our] selection. When **Lady Gregory** was here the last time, lecturing, she told me one day, half in earnest and half in fun, that if she died in this country she wanted to be buried where she died,

Pittsburgh, 1912, when Lady Gregory visited with The Abbey Theatre

> unless she died in Pittsburgh. She refused to be buried in Pittsburgh... One day downtown, when I was having coffee after lunch with two or three men, one of them said: 'Times change. Now there is [famous actress] Lillian Russell. In the old days she was supposed to have had many lovers and she was married and divorced four or five times. But years go by, and she marries again, and settles down, and finally dies in the odor of—'

'Pittsburgh,' said I.

Lady Gregory refused to be buried in the odor of Pittsburgh."

Quinn ends by congratulating **Yeats** on his honorary degree from Trinity College and asks that **Willie's** wife send him some photos of their children and Thoor Ballylee, the tower they are living in.

Now he is ready to pack up and go on a well-earned vacation.

❧ AUGUST 4, 1922 ❧
6:25 PM EST, AMERICA

Telephone service throughout the country is suspended for one minute to mark the funeral of Alexander Graham Bell, the Scottish-born engineer who patented the first practical telephone 46 years ago.

Bell died of complications from diabetes and pernicious anemia two days ago at his home in Nova Scotia at age 75.

New York Daily News, *August 2*

❧ AUGUST 8, 1922 ❧
LINCOLN GARDENS, EAST 31ST STREET; AND
COTTAGE GROVE AVENUE, CHICAGO, ILLINOIS

Standing outside the Lincoln Gardens cabaret, listening to the jazz band inside, cornet player Louis Armstrong, just turned 21 and just arrived from New Orleans, is too intimidated to go inside.

Lincoln Gardens advertisement

The band leader, Joe "King" Oliver, 40, who he knew a bit from back home, had invited Louis by telegram to come and join his Creole Jazz Band. Oliver was supposed to meet him at the Illinois Central Station tonight. When the train was late, Oliver paid a porter to get Armstrong here in a taxi so he could sit in for some of the set.

Now Louis is hesitating. They sure sound good.

Suddenly King Oliver comes out the door and shouts at Armstrong,

 Come on IN HEAH you little dumb sumbitch. We've been waiting for your black ass all night."

King Oliver's Creole Jazz Band

Armstrong goes in.

When the band is done, Oliver takes his new band member home with him, and his wife feeds him some familiar New Orleans food. Armstrong can't believe it when Oliver takes him to a one-bedroom apartment—with bath!—that they have arranged for him on Wabash Avenue. All this and $52 a week, too…

❧ AUGUST **10, 1922** ❧
LIFE MAGAZINE, NEW YORK CITY, NEW YORK

L*ife* magazine's weekly listings section includes capsule reviews of current plays, written by their theatre critic, **Robert Benchley**, 32:

❝ *Abie's Irish Rose*. Republic Theatre—Something awful.❞

❧ EARLY AUGUST, 1922 ❧
GLASGOW, SCOTLAND; AND
PRESBYTERIAN HOSPITAL, NEW YORK CITY, NEW YORK

At first, American actor and singer Paul Robeson, 24, was really enjoying his first trip to the UK, touring with a production of *Voodoo* by Mary Hoyt Wiborg, 34. He had appeared in the Broadway premiere—when it was called *Taboo*—and Miss Wiborg had used her posh connections to arrange a British tour starring none other than the legendary Mrs. Patrick Campbell, 57.

Mrs. Pat, as she is known, has been impressed with Paul's talents—he was thought by many to be the only good thing in the original show.

Mrs. Patrick Campbell

She edited the play to make his part better, and, after she heard him humming "Go Down Moses" when he was preparing for a dream sequence, she insisted that he add more singing. During one of the curtain calls, Mrs. Pat pushed Paul forward, saying to him,

❝   It's your show—not mine"

as the audience's applause increased. She has mentioned to Robeson that he would make a great Othello.

But their opening in Blackpool was a disappointment; the show didn't get any better in Edinburgh. There was some improvement last night, here in Glasgow. And Paul got another good review:

❝ Particularly good was Mr. Paul Robson [sic] as the minstrel Jim…
[He] sang and acted splendidly…a magnificent voice, his singing has
undoubtedly much to do with the success *Voodoo* achieved last night.”

Robeson has been to a Celtics v. Hibernians “football” match, and generally
found he is treated better here as a Black man than he is back in the States.

Now things seem to be turning sour. Mrs. Campbell is mumbling about
leaving the show and shutting it down before they get to London.

More worrying to Paul, though, is the correspondence he’s been getting from
his wife of one year, Essie, 26, back in New York.

He writes to her almost every day, with great detail about the show and
his experiences:

❝ Mrs. Pat is a really wonderful woman and a marvelous actress…
[English theatre] seems in as bad a state as those in New York or
worse…Vaudeville pays better here than the *legitimate*…”

Paul receives letters from her regularly. But they seem odd. Essie doesn’t
respond to what he has told her, and doesn’t answer his questions about their
future: Does she want to join him over here? Maybe he should think about
going to Oxford University for a year? Or should he finish law school back
at Columbia in New York? What’s the best plan that will give them a solid
foundation for their life together?

Paul writes to Essie that he has too many options.

❝ Worries me sick…[You should] think carefully from every angle…
You’ll know what to do…You always know.”

❧⚘❧

Back in New York City, Essie is in Presbyterian Hospital where she works as a chemist in the Surgical Pathology Department. But now she is a patient.

The day before Paul left for the UK, back in July, Essie's doctor told her she needed an immediate operation to correct complications from her recent appendectomy.

Essie didn't want Paul to worry about her while he was away, so she waited until his ship pulled out of New York harbor and then checked herself into Presby.

Essie had written out 21 letters to him in advance and handed them over to friends whom she could trust to mail them to him at regular intervals.

The operation went fine, but Essie developed phlebitis and other complications, so the doctors have kept her in here longer than anticipated.

Essie loves the beautiful letters she receives from her husband. She's thinking it might be time to send Paul a telegram and tell him the truth.

❦ AUGUST, 1922 ❧
NEW YORK CITY, NEW YORK;
DUBLIN; AND LONDON

In America, Ireland and England, many are still working their way through *Ulysses*.

In the States, Gilbert Seldes, 29, writes in *The Nation*,

❝ Today [James Joyce] has brought forth *Ulysses*…a monstrous and magnificent travesty, which makes him possibly the most interesting and the most formidable of our time…I think that Nietzsche would have cared for the tragic gaiety of *Ulysses*."

❦❧

In Dublin, poet and artist **AE** [**George Russell**, 55] writes to his friend in New York City, Irish-American lawyer John Quinn, 52:

❝ I see the ability and mastery while not liking the mood…[Joyce is] very Irish…The Irish genius is coming out of its seclusion and **[W. B.] Yeats**, **[John Millington] Synge**, **[George] Moore**, [George Bernard] Shaw, Joyce and others are forerunners. The Irish imagination is virgin soil and virgin soil is immensely productive when cultivated. We are devotees of convention in normal circumstances and when we break away we outrage convention."

Another Irish friend, novelist and poet James Stephens, 42, writes to Quinn that he didn't even bother to try *Ulysses*.

❝ It is too expensive to buy and too difficult to borrow, and too long to read, and, from what I have heard about it, altogether too difficult to talk about."

❧❦❧

In London, novelist **Virginia Woolf**, 40, has been working on a short story, "Mrs. Dalloway in Bond Street" while still trying to get through *Ulysses*. She admits to her diary,

❝ I should be reading *Ulysses*, & fabricating my case for & against. I have read 200 pages. So far—not a third; & have been amused, stimulated, charmed interested by the first two or three chapters—to the end of the Cemetery scene…And Tom [American ex-pat poet T. S. Eliot], great Tom, thinks this on a par with *War & Peace*! An illiterate, underbred book it seems to me: the book of a self-taught working man, & we all know how distressing they are, how egotistic, insistent, raw, striking, & ultimately nauseating. When 1 can have the cooked flesh, why have the raw? But I think if you are anemic, as Tom is, there is glory in blood. Being fairly normal myself I am soon ready for the classics again. I may revise this later. I do not compromise my critical sagacity. I plant a stick in the ground to mark page 200…I dislike *Ulysses* more & more—that is I think it more & more unimportant: & don't even trouble conscientiously to make out its meanings. Thank God, I need not write about it."

But **Virginia** does write about it to her Bloomsbury friend, biographer and essayist **Lytton Strachey**, 42:

❝ Never did I read such tosh. As for the first two chapters we will let them pass, but the 3rd 4th 5th 6th–merely the scratching of pimples on the body of the bootboy at Claridges. Of course genius may blaze out on page 652 but I have my doubts. And this is what Eliot worships…"

🎗 AUGUST 17, 1922 🎗
LIFE MAGAZINE, NEW YORK CITY, NEW YORK

L*ife* magazine's weekly listings section includes capsule reviews of current plays, written by their theatre critic, **Robert Benchley**, 32:

" " *Abie's Irish Rose*. Republic Theatre—Couldn't be much worse."

❧ AUGUST, 1922 ❧
PHOTOPLAY MAGAZINE, LOS ANGELES, CALIFORNIA; AND NEW YORK CITY, NEW YORK

"Cal York," writing under the pseudonym formed by the two locations of the main editorial offices of *Photoplay* magazine, asks:

Rudolph Valentino in Blood and Sand

    ❝ Is Rudolph Valentino wearing a wig in *Blood and Sand,* or did he permit his slick hair to be coiffed into the curly mop you see under this Spanish cap? Cheer up—it's only temporary. Later on in the picture he looks more like Julio [his character in the hit, *Four Horsemen of the Apocalypse*]."

❧ AUGUST 24, 1922 ❧
MONK'S HOUSE, RODMELL, EAST SUSSEX, ENGLAND

Writing in her diary, writer **Virginia Woolf**, 40, notes that,

❝ I open the paper and find Michael Collins dead in a ditch."

Collins, 32, the Commander-in-Chief of Ireland's National Army, was assassinated two days ago by a sniper while taking the risk of traveling through County Cork, which is under the control of the opposition forces, led by Eamon de Valera, 39.

Woolf is about to launch her third novel, *Jacob's Room*, and is also working on a short story, "Mrs. Dalloway in Bond Street." And she is still struggling to get through *Ulysses* by Irish writer James Joyce, 40.

Today, however, she is responding to a letter from an old friend, telling her that Katherine Mansfield, 33, is back in London, staying in Hampstead.

Woolf greatly admires Mansfield. The Hogarth Press, which **Virginia** operates with her husband **Leonard**, 41, out of their London home, published Mansfield's short story *Prelude* when they first started their company four years ago; it has sold over 200 copies.

But **Virginia** also looks at Katherine as one of her main rivals. Her current collection, *The Garden Party and Other Stories*, which Hogarth lost to a more mainstream publisher, "soars in the newspapers & runs up sales skyhigh" as **Virginia** wrote in her diary.

Katherine has been mostly away from London for the past two years, undergoing experimental treatments in France and Switzerland to treat her tuberculosis. Before returning to London a few weeks ago she wrote another short story. And her will.

Staying in Hampstead with painter Dorothy Brett, 38, an old acquaintance of her husband, Katherine has kept to her room, hanging a sign on the door telling visitors to stay away as she is working. She ventures out to attend lectures about the effect on your body of having a "diseased spirit," and to have experimental radiation treatments.

Dorothy Brett

Dorothy has invited **Virginia** to join them at one of the regular salons she holds on Thursday evenings in the posh Hampstead house her parents have bought for her. She feels **Virginia** and Katherine would appreciate the opportunity to see each other again.

As **Virginia** writes to her old friend, she "agonized" over the invitation. It would be great to see people again, back in the city. But would the trip to London just distract her from what she is working on?

Virginia decides she will pass on the salon and make a point to see Katherine next summer when she's back in town.

❧ LATE AUGUST, 1922 ❧
74 GLOUCESTER PLACE, MARYLEBONE, LONDON

While English novelist **Virginia Woolf**, 40, in Rodmell, East Sussex, is struggling to get past page 200 of *Ulysses*, the book's author, James Joyce, also 40, is about 70 miles north, here in Marylebone, London, meeting one of his key benefactors, publisher Harriet Shaw Weaver, 45, for the first time.

Joyce and Weaver have been corresponding for years; she published his work in her *Egoist* magazine and his books with her Egoist Press, in addition to supporting him substantially with stipends from her late mother's inherited money.

Recent treatment Joyce has been receiving for his painful iritis seems to be working, so he decided this would be a good time to make the trip over from his home in Paris with his partner, Nora Barnacle, 38.

When the Joyces arrived here at Harriet's home, she noticed that he was well-dressed and had excellent manners, but that his huge spectacles accentuate the terrible state that his eyes are in. He and Nora both impressed her with their Irish charm.

Harriet is a bit concerned that the Joyces are going all over town by taxi—even Harriet rides the bus sometimes. He blows about £200 in the month they are here.

Weaver hadn't realized until recently just how much personal care Joyce's Paris publisher, American Sylvia Beach, 35, owner of the Shakespeare and Company bookstore, has been providing for him. In addition to publishing *Ulysses* this past February, Sylvia has been helping to support the family and making sure Joyce is seeing eye specialists.

Now, toward the end of their trip, Joyce is having a relapse. Harriet arranges a visit to her own eye doctor who, like the French physicians, advises immediate surgery. Joyce figures it's a good time to head back home to Paris.

(Photo by Topical Press Agency/Getty Images)

London taxis and buses

Before he and Nora leave, however, they visit with one of his Irish relatives who works here in London. Joyce asks her what her mother back in Ireland thinks of his novel, *Ulysses*, and she says,

❝   Well, Jim, mother thought it was not fit to read."

To which Joyce replies,

❝   If *Ulysses* isn't fit to read, life isn't fit to live."

August 30, 1922
RAF Recruiting Office, Henrietta Street, Covent Garden, London

A young blonde man walks into the recruiting office and fills out an application to enlist in the Royal Air Force. John Hume Ross, 28.

Except he isn't.

He is Thomas Edward Lawrence, just turned 34, former colonel in the British Army, known for his role in the Arab revolt against the Ottoman Empire during the Great War, and until recently a bored bureaucrat in the government's Foreign Office.

Even though his supervisor there, Winston Churchill, 47, head of the Colonial Office and MP for Dundee, sent him back to the Middle East several times, Lawrence found the administrative work stultifying. Churchill finally accepted his resignation last month.

Secretary Winston Churchill on the job

Since the end of the War, Lawrence has been working on his memoir, *Seven Pillars of Wisdom*, and privately published, at his own expense, a few copies with the Oxford Press this summer.

During his service he realized how important air power now is in battle; he wants to re-enlist, this time with the RAF.

Anticipating problems if he tries to sign up at his age, earlier this year Lawrence met with Sir Hugh Trenchard, 49, the "father" of the RAF, at the Air Ministry to tell him of his plan. Trenchard agreed.

Now, at the recruiting office, Flying Officer W. E. Johns, 29, is suspicious of "Ross" and his fitness for service. Lawrence admits that he gave false information and Johns rejects him.

Lawrence contacts Trenchard who sends a message that Officer Johns must accept Lawrence.

He's in. Again.

❧ SEPTEMBER, 1922 ❧
CAFÉ DE FLORE,
CORNER OF BOULEVARD SAINT-GERMAIN AND
RUE SAINT-BENOIT, PARIS

Three American women are seated at the little marble-topped tables in front of the café. Each is wearing a black tailored suit, a white satin scarf, and white gloves. One wears a black cloak.

Each has a martini on the table in front of her. All three are writers.

Café de Flore

Djuna Barnes, 30, from Croton-on-Hudson, New York, wearing her signature cloak, has been living in Paris since last year. Her lengthy profile of Irish writer James Joyce, 40, caused quite a stir when it was published in *Vanity Fair* a few months ago.

Solita Solano, 33, born Sarah Wilkinson in Troy, New York, also an established writer, has just moved to the city with her lover, Janet Flanner, 30, from Indianapolis, Indiana, so they both can work on their novels.

When they first arrived earlier this month, Solano and Flanner took rooms in a small pension on rue de Quatrefages. But the constant noise was annoying. Drowning out the dedicated piano student practicing down the hall was the construction crew renovating a mosque down the street.

They have now moved to two small fifth-floor rooms, Nos. 15 and 16, in the Hotel Napoleon Bonaparte, 36 rue Bonaparte, each paying one dollar a day for the relative quiet. They are near the cafés and L'Ecole des Beaux-Arts.

In addition to the Flore, one of their other regular haunts is a neighborhood restaurant, La Quatrieme Republique, named in anticipation of a fourth French Republic following the current one. A few doors from their hotel, the restaurant's food is interesting and affordable. However, they have nicknamed their usual waitress "Yvonne the Terrible" for her shrewish demeanor, despite their generous tips.

Solano and Flanner met after the Great War back in New York City. Flanner and her husband discovered after they had moved there that they had nothing in common, so they separated. He was happy with his boring bank; Janet hung out in Greenwich Village with bohemians, in Harlem with jazz musicians, and in midtown with writers and artists. At parties in the studio owned by illustrator Neysa McMein, 34, Flanner became friends with a young couple, magazine editor **Harold Ross**, 29, and his wife, *New York Times* reporter Jane Grant, 30.

And she also met Solita.

They fell in love and when Solano, the drama critic for the *New York Tribune*, was offered a commission from *National Geographic* to tour the Mediterranean and Middle East, sending back stories, she brought Janet along.

After a year of travel, they have now decided to settle here in Paris, living off their writings and a bit of money Flanner's father left her, and begin serious work on their novels.

Janet sends letters from Paris back to Grant in New York, chronicling the daily life of the ex-pats in the City of Light.

❧ EARLY SEPTEMBER, 1922 ❧
31 NASSAU STREET, NEW YORK CITY, NEW YORK

After dinner in Paris many months ago.

After cables from publisher to author and author to lawyer.

After phone calls from lawyer to publisher.

After numerous letters from author to lawyer to editors to publishers.

Finally, corporate attorney, supporter of artists and writers, John Quinn, 52, has managed to get Horace Liveright, 37, owner of Boni and Liveright publishing company, and Gilbert Seldes, 29, managing editor of *The Dial* magazine, sitting together here in his law office to work out who is going to be first to publish *The Waste Land*, the latest poem by T. S. Eliot, 33, living in London.

Liveright first expressed interest when he was introduced to Eliot by another American ex-pat poet, Ezra Pound, 36, in Paris over dinner at the beginning of the year.

Boni and Liveright logo for Modern Library series

They began corresponding and Liveright was interested in publishing the poem but concerned it wouldn't be long enough to be a book on its own. Quinn wanted Eliot to add four or five more poems, but Eliot refused.

The Dial magazine has published Eliot's poetry before, and he has been writing a "London Letter" column for them when he is feeling up to it.

Seldes and one of the owners, James Sibley Watson, Jr., 28, are both keen to have "The Waste Land" debut in *The Dial*. But the other owner, Scofield Thayer, 32, currently living in Vienna, is not impressed with Eliot or his work.

Eliot estimates that the finished poem will be 450 lines. Figuring 35 to 40 lines to a printed page, and standard payment of $10 per page for poetry, paid upon acceptance, and adding in a little extra, Thayer offered Eliot a generous $150. Eliot was not impressed. He cabled that he wanted $250.

Thayer hadn't seen the poem yet but wrote to his staff that it might be a good thing if they don't get to publish it. He'd rather publish classics like Edith Wharton, 60, who currently has a hit novel, *The Glimpses of the Moon.*

John Quinn *by John Butler Yeats*

But Seldes is worried that he doesn't have enough material for his upcoming issues, and so he wants to get this agreement nailed down.

Pound assured Thayer, by letter, that "The Waste Land" is Eliot's best work. And he has pulled it off while working full-time at a bank and nursing a depressed wife.

Meanwhile, Liveright mailed Eliot a contract for publishing the book—and he didn't like those terms either. He asked Quinn to negotiate for him, giving him power of attorney to make whatever decision he felt best.

Quinn is happy to help because he likes Eliot. He's not always begging Quinn for money the way Irish novelist James Joyce, 40, does.

Quinn received the typescript from Eliot at the end of July, read it, had it typed up professionally, and sent it over to Liveright—although at that point he couldn't remember what the final title was—before leaving on a month-long vacation in the Adirondacks.

Now he is back in his office, well rested, facing the editor of the only magazine that wants to publish "The Waste Land" and the owner of the only book publishing company that wants to publish it.

Why has it taken so long?!

Quinn and Seldes convince Liveright that the best plan is to publish the poem in *The Dial* first, in the November issue which will be on newsstands around October 20.

To entice Eliot, Seldes promises that the magazine will also announce in the December issue that the poet will receive the second annual Dial award of $2,000, in addition to the regular fee of $150.

Boni and Liveright will then follow up with publication of *The Waste Land* as a book before the end of the year, with copious notes which Eliot is adding, that won't be in the magazine version. They will pay him $150 upfront plus royalties.

The Dial also agrees to buy 350 copies of the $2 book version, at a 40% discount, to use as promotional items for subscribers, thereby guaranteeing that Boni and Liveright won't lose money on the deal.

Everyone agrees to keep the news about the Dial Prize a secret until it is officially announced in the magazine. Then they all sign the agreement and go to lunch.

❧ FALL, 1922 ❧
DETROIT AND WINDSOR FERRYPORT,
DETROIT, MICHIGAN

Phew. He made it.

Barnet Braverman, 34, former radical newspaper editor turned boring advertising guy, has just crossed the border from Canada into the United States carrying one copy of the recently published novel *Ulysses* by Irishman James Joyce, 40, which has been banned in this country for being obscene.

If he'd been caught, he faced a $5,000 fine and up to five years in prison.

Earlier this year Barnet had been contacted by the publisher of the controversial novel, American Sylvia Beach, 35, who operates a bookstore in Paris, Shakespeare and Company. One of the young aspiring novelists who hangs out in her store, **Ernest Hemingway**, 23, had suggested Braverman, whom he'd known when they both worked in advertising in Chicago.

Braverman is excited and proud to take part in this international literary smuggling ring. He wants to stick it to the short-sighted American publishers who refused to publish *Ulysses* and also put one over on the censors he refers to as "Methodist smut hounds."

So far everything has gone to plan. For $35 a month Braverman rented a small room near the office where he works in Windsor, Ontario. He told the landlord that he's in the publishing business.

Sylvia then shipped 40 copies of the book to his Canadian address. That's when he had to deal with the Canadian customs officials.

Canada hasn't gotten around to banning *Ulysses* yet. But their duty is 25% of the value of any printed material, which would mean $300. With some fast talking, Braverman convinced the customs officer that these 700-page books, printed on fine paper, are only worth 50 cents each. So he only had to pay $6.50 for the lot and then store the books in his rented room.

Once he gets them into the States, Braverman will send *Ulysses* to American customers COD so that the private express messenger company has to deliver them to get paid. And this plan avoids sending "obscene" material through the U.S. mail.

After work today, Braverman picked up one copy, wrapped it up, and carried it under his arm onto the ferry. When he got off in Detroit, he unwrapped it for the border officer there, who waved him through with no problem.

Now Barnet just has to do that 39 more times.

❧ SEPTEMBER 8, 1922 ❧
ATLANTIC CITY, NEW JERSEY

Competing against 57 other women in the "Intercity" category, recent high school graduate, Miss Columbus, Ohio, Mary Katherine Campbell, 17 (or so she says), is crowned the winner of the second annual Miss America pageant, sponsored by the Atlantic City Businessmen's League to increase business on the Boardwalk.

Miss America, Mary Katherine Campbell

Campbell is awarded $5,000 and the Golden Mermaid Trophy; she is already enrolled as an art major at Ohio State University.

❧ SEPTEMBER 12, 1922 ❧
MANHATTAN MUNICIPAL TERM COURT,
NEW YORK CITY, NEW YORK; AND
NEAR TAOS, NEW MEXICO

City Magistrate George W. Simpson, 51, is issuing his decision in the case brought against publisher Thomas A. Seltzer, 47, by John Sumner, 45, head of the New York Society for the Suppression of Vice (NYSSV), for publishing three "obscene" books, including the novel *Women in Love* by English writer D. H. Lawrence, just turned 37 yesterday.

Based on his own reading, as well as expert testimony from critics such as Gilbert Seldes, 29, managing editor of *The Dial* magazine—who testified that the novel "would not interest a child and be no more exciting to an adult than a railroad timetable"—Simpson dismisses all charges and orders that the confiscated books be returned to the publisher.

Echoing a decision issued just 10 days earlier in the case *Halsey v. NYSSV*, Simpson states that

❝ Mere extracts separated from their context do not constitute criteria by which books might be judged obscene,"

and that the books in question have value as literature.

Seltzer's attorney announces that they will bring suit against Sumner and the NYSSV. And Seltzer knows that sales will soar.

❧❧

The author in question, D. H. Lawrence, arrived with his wife, Frieda, 43, at their new home in Taos, New Mexico, just yesterday. What a birthday present.

After more than a year of correspondence between the two, Lawrence finally met his hostess, Mabel Dodge, 43, when he and Frieda stepped off the train yesterday in Lamy, New Mexico, 90 miles south.

Dodge, swathed in turquoise and dripping silver jewelry, was accompanied by her partner, a rather silent Native American Tony Luhan, 43, who drove them here to Taos in Mabel's Cadillac.

Dodge has fixed up a roomy house for the Lawrences, just 200 yards away from the one she shares with Luhan, about a mile from the town's central plaza.

Lawrence is impressed with their new surroundings. But early this morning, he has gone to Mabel's house to begin working with her on the novel she wants him to write. She invites him to come up to her roof terrace where she is sunbathing. Passing through her bedroom, Lawrence sees her unmade bed and instinctively makes a disgusted face, which Mabel sees. She is disappointed that the author she has put so much faith in is so small-minded.

Lawrence tells Mabel that his wife doesn't want them working together at Mabel's house; there is plenty of room for them at the Lawrences'. So Dodge and Lawrence gather round the table there.

Frieda makes a point of stomping around the house while loudly sweeping and singing.

❧ SEPTEMBER 14, 1922 ❧
LIFE MAGAZINE, NEW YORK CITY, NEW YORK

*L*ife magazine's weekly listings section includes capsule reviews of current plays, written by their theatre critic, **Robert Benchley**, 32:

> " *Abie's Irish Rose*. Republic Theatre—People laugh at this every night, which explains why a democracy can never be a success."

❧ SEPTEMBER 16, 1922 ❧
NEW YORK CITY, NEW YORK

Don't wear white after Labor Day! And, gentlemen, don't wear a straw hat after September 15! Marauding hooligans in New York City may knock it off your head and stomp it on the ground. Or worse!

A sea of straw hats

No one is sure where this tradition started, but men are supposed to switch to their winter felt hats on September 15 or face the fashion police. This year, a group of young thugs started early, a few days ago, knocking the straw hats off dock workers coming off their shift. The dock workers fought back.

Traffic on the Manhattan Bridge was stopped and arrests were made.

Today's headline in the *New York Tribune* is

❝ Straw Hat Smashing Orgy Bares Heads from Battery to Bronx."

The *New York Times* goes with

❝ City Has Wild Night of Straw Hat Riots:

Gangs of Young Hoodlums with Spike Sticks Terrorize Whole Blocks."

❧ MID-SEPTEMBER, 1922 ❧
MONK'S HOUSE, RODMELL, EAST SUSSEX; AND GARSINGTON, OXFORDSHIRE, ENGLAND

Looking back, the weekend was a bit awkward.

Novelist **Virginia Woolf**, 40, and her husband **Leonard**, 41, hosted their last house guests for this summer.

Fellow novelist Edward Morgan Forster, 43, arrived on Friday evening, carrying only a fraying backpack for luggage and dressed in old clothes.

American ex-pat poet Thomas Stearns Eliot, about to turn 34, didn't come until Saturday afternoon, after finishing his day job at Lloyds Bank in the morning. He was dressed a bit more formally.

Morgan kept to himself most of the weekend, writing in his room. **Virginia** realized that Forster does better when he is the only weekend guest, not having to mix too much with others he's not comfortable around.

What was most interesting about the weekend was what was *not* talked about.

Eliot never mentioned the long poem he's been working on, which he had read to the **Woolfs** a few months ago. Although they did talk about a fund that fellow American ex-pat poet Ezra Pound, 36, living in France, is trying to set up for Eliot so he can leave his bank job. Eliot seems a bit embarrassed by the effort.

Virginia is also a bit envious of Morgan's confidence over the novel he's been working on.

❝ He is happy in his novel, but does not want to discuss it,"

she writes in her diary.

And no one mentioned the recent coverage of an extensive report by the War Office Committee which, for two years, has been looking into "shell shock" in veterans from the Great War. It is causing quite a stir. One recommendation is that the medical term be changed to "war neurosis" as some who served never really heard shells.

On Sunday afternoon, after tea, Eliot leaves. The whole atmosphere changes. As **Virginia** records in her diary, she, **Leonard** and Morgan,

❝ snuggled in & Morgan became very familiar; anecdotic; simple, gossiping about friends & humming his little tunes."

❊❊❊

Meanwhile, one of **Virginia's** Bloomsbury friends, biographer **Lytton Strachey**, 42, has written to her about a "not very stimulating" weekend he is having at Garsington, the country home of former Liberal MP Philip Morrell, 52, and his wife Ottoline, 49. **Lytton** describes his hostess to **Virginia** in less than flattering terms:

❝ Ottoline was dreadfully *degringole* [tumbling down in my opinion]…: her bladder has now gone the way of her wits—a melancholy dribble; and then, as she sits after dinner in the lamplight, her cheek pouches

Lady Ottoline Morrell

drooping with peppermints, a cigarette between her false teeth, and vast spectacles on her painted nose, the effect produced is extremely agitating. I found I want to howl like an Irish wolf—but perhaps the result produced in you was different."

❧ SEPTEMBER **21, 1922** ❧
LIFE MAGAZINE, NEW YORK CITY, NEW YORK

L*ife* magazine's weekly listings section includes capsule reviews of current plays, written by their theatre critic, **Robert Benchley**, 32:

> ❝*Abie's Irish Rose*. Republic Theatre—Showing that people will laugh at anything."

⚘ LATE SEPTEMBER, 1922 ⚘
23 RUE DE BOITIE; AND MORGAN, HARJES ET CIE, 14 PLACE VENDOME, PARIS

Olga Picasso, 31, is recuperating at home after an emergency operation.

She and her family—husband Pablo, 40, and their son, Paulo, almost 20 months old—were having a lovely holiday, despite the bad weather, in Dinard on the Brittany Coast.

Suddenly Olga became seriously ill and they had to rush her to the hospital in Paris, 400 km away. The five-hour trip was a nightmare: Paolo was car sick and Pablo kept putting ice packs on Olga's head.

She's feeling a bit better now that she is home. But Pablo has gone back to Dinard to retrieve all the paintings and drawings he's been working on since they arrived there in July.

The Spanish painter has never learned to drive, saying that it would affect his wrists and hands. So he bought a posh new car and has hired a chauffeur to take care of the driving for him. He tells Olga that, back in Dinard, he is quite a celebrity. His arrival is in the local paper and everyone wants to see his new car.

Olga is more concerned about her "woman's problems."

⚘⚘

Nearby in the city, about two km away, American ex-patriate Harry Crosby, 24, is at his desk in the Morgan, Harjes et Cie bank in Place Vendome.

Harry's not doing much work. He rarely does. His aunt, Jane Norton Morgan, 54, wife of the bank owner, J. P. Morgan, Jr., just turned 55, arranged this job

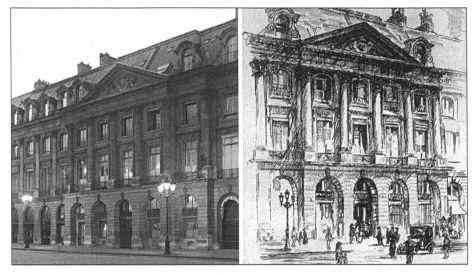

Morgan, Harjes et Cie bank in Place Vendome

for him. Harry had already walked out on a banking job in Boston, after only eight months of putting up with it and a six-day drinking binge.

But Aunt Jane didn't send him off to Paris this spring just to restart his career. She wanted to get him away from his mistress, Mrs. Mary "Polly" Phelps Rodgers, 30, with whom he has been conducting a scandalous affair for the past two years. All of Boston is talking.

Didn't work. Polly finally divorced her husband earlier this year, and at the beginning of this month she finally said yes to Harry's most recent marriage proposal, via transatlantic cable.

Harry was over the moon. He collected on the $100 bet he'd made with his roommate, raced to Cherbourg to get the next boat, used the money to bribe officials so he wouldn't have to quarantine, and managed to sail to New York City on the *RMS Aquitania* on 3rd September. He won some money gambling on the ship but used that to buy champagne for his fellow passengers. He dressed up and crashed the posh restaurant on board, but while he was eating caviar, mock turtle soup and hummingbirds on toast, a steerage inspector tossed him out.

Harry arrived in Manhattan after six days at sea, broke, and Polly was waiting for him at the dock. They got married that day and made a quick trip to Washington, D. C., to try to reconcile with his family. That didn't work.

Back in New York City they collected Polly's two children, and the responsibility of actually being a stepfather sunk in to Harry. He disappeared for a few hours.

But all four members of the newly blended family boarded the *RMS Aquitania* for the trip back to Paris.

Harry returned to this cushy job, and Polly found them an impressive apartment on the Right Bank so they could move out of the hotel they had been living in. And every workday, Polly, in a stunning red bathing suit, rows her new husband—somberly dressed in a business suit, hat, umbrella and briefcase—down the Seine to Place de la Concorde. He disembarks and walks the few blocks to his job here at the family bank. Polly rows back, often to the delight of the Frenchmen who whistle and wave at her and her large breasts. She loves it.

Harry likes this life, too, but not the job. He spends a lot of time reading poetry rather than banking and has even tried writing some himself.

Right now, he thinks it's time to leave this office and go across the street to the Ritz Hotel Bar.

❧ LATE SEPTEMBER, ❧ EARLY OCTOBER, 1922
82 MERRION SQUARE, DUBLIN; AND GREAT NECK, LONG ISLAND, NEW YORK

Georgie Yeats, 29, is relieved to be settling into her new home in Merrion Square, Dublin, with her family—her husband, poet **William Butler Yeats**, 57, and their two children, Anne, three, and Michael, 13 months.

She bought the lease on this posh row house just a few months ago, with her own family money. But they have been living out in the west of Ireland, in the tower **Willie** bought and named Thoor Ballylee.

Willie has been optimistic about how the newly independent Irish Free State is progressing. Despite the ongoing Civil War, the Parliament elected in June has taken their seats and chosen W. T. Cosgrave, 42, as their President.

However, at the beginning of this month Republican soldiers came to the door of Thoor Ballylee and told Georgie that they were going to blow up the bridge over the stream that runs by the tower. She should move the family upstairs. Big of them to give notice.

They ignited the fuses; a Republican told her there would be two explosions. She writes to a friend:

❝   After two minutes, two roars came & then a hail of falling masonry & gravel & then the same man shouted up 'All right now' & cleared off."

No one was injured. When the **Yeats** family left for Dublin the stream had poured two feet of water in the downstairs dining room.

❧❧

Zelda and Scott Fitzgerald

As she got off the train at Great Neck, Long Island, Zelda Fitzgerald, 22, carrying her daughter Scottie, 11 months, took one look at the nanny that her husband, hit novelist **F. Scott Fitzgerald**, just turned 26, had hired and fired her.

Scott and Zelda have recently rented a house in this suburb, only a 45-minute drive from Manhattan, and while Zelda went back to St. Paul, Minnesota, to pick up Scottie from **Fitzgerald's** parents, **Scott** had botched things up as usual.

They had come back to New York at the beginning of the month to start a life with less booze and more work on **Scott's** next novel and a play he's writing. But they made the mistake of staying in their favorite place for partying, the Plaza Hotel, and the partying came back too.

A few weeks ago, **Scott** invited his old Princeton University buddy, critic and managing editor of *Vanity Fair*, Edmund "Bunny" Wilson, 27, over to the Plaza for an impromptu lunch—lobster croquettes and top shelf illegal liquor. Also joining them were novelists John Dos Passos, 26, and **Sherwood Anderson**, 46, who was looking a bit scruffy. The bootlegger's bartender mixed Bronx cocktails (gin, vermouth and orange juice) and the men sat around drinking and whining about how their publishers don't promote their books enough.

Dos Passos and Zelda started teasing each other and **Anderson**, who had only come to be polite, left early.

Scott mentioned that, now that he had published two successful novels and just brought out his second short story collection, *Tales of the Jazz Age*, he and Zelda had decided to rent a house out on Long Island where they could raise their daughter.

So the slightly tipsy **Fitzgeralds** and Dos Passos got in a chauffeured red touring car and took off to meet up with a real estate agent in Great Neck. None of the houses interested them so they decided to pay a call on their friend, humor writer Ring Lardner, 37, at his home on East Shore Road looking out over Manhasset Bay.

Ring was already drunker than they were, so after only a few more drinks the group headed back to the Plaza. Zelda insisted on stopping at an amusement park along the way so she could ride the Ferris Wheel, and Scott stayed in the car drinking from a bottle that he had hidden there. Dos Passos decided his new friends were going to have a hard time adjusting to strictly domestic life.

After several other house-hunting trips, the **Fitzgeralds** finally found this lovely home at 6 Gateway Drive, in the leafy confines of Great Neck Estates: A circular driveway; red-tiled roof; great big pine tree in the front yard; and a room above the garage where **Scott** can write in peace.

Zelda took off to retrieve Scottie in St. Paul, leaving **Fitzgerald** to hire servants and a baby nurse. He sure has screwed that up.

Despite his recent writing success, and encouragement from his publisher, **Scott** really isn't making enough to afford the rent, the servants, the laundress, the nurse, the country club, the theatre tickets, the restaurant bills, and the Rolls Royce (second hand) that living in Great Neck requires.

Zelda doesn't care. The finances are his problem.

❧ LATE SEPTEMBER, 1922 ❧
PRESBYTERIAN HOSPITAL,
NEW YORK CITY, NEW YORK

What?! When American actor Paul Robeson, 24, in London, received the cable from his wife of one year, Essie Goode Robeson, 26, back in New York City, he couldn't believe it.

Paul had been touring the UK in a play, *Voodoo*—called *Taboo* when he premiered it in the US—with legendary English actress Mrs. Patrick Campbell, 57. He'd been writing letters home to Essie almost every day, but the ones he received from her seemed remote, with no comments regarding all the details he was giving her about his life here. Finally, he cabled her,

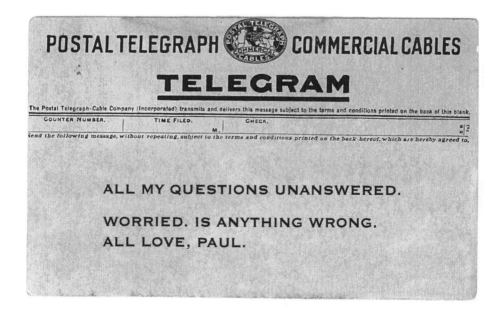

POSTAL TELEGRAPH ☆ COMMERCIAL CABLES

TELEGRAM

The Postal Telegraph-Cable Company (Incorporated) transmits and delivers this message subject to the terms and conditions printed on the back of this blank.

COUNTER NUMBER.		TIME FILED.		CHECK.		
			M.			

Send the following message, without repeating, subject to the terms and conditions printed on the back hereof, which are hereby agreed to.

ALL MY QUESTIONS UNANSWERED.

WORRIED. IS ANYTHING WRONG.
ALL LOVE, PAUL.

Something sure was wrong—Essie replied that she had been in the hospital the whole time! She hadn't told him about the complications from her appendectomy, and she'd checked herself in right after he left for the UK. Essie had written out letters to him in advance and had friends send them to Paul at regular intervals so he wouldn't worry. Ha,

Paul wrote back to say he will return home right away. The producers of the play have decided not to take it on to London, so Paul books a ticket on the *RMS Homeric*.

As soon as he docks in New York City, Robeson goes straight to Presbyterian Hospital where Essie, now a patient, has worked for years, even before her marriage, as a chemist in the Surgical Pathology Department. When Paul asks to see his wife, Essie, the receptionist says,

❝ Oh, you're Mr. Goode; I'll take you right up!"

Reunited, Paul vows to stay by her side in the hospital until she is ready to go home to their house in Harlem to recuperate.

❧ OCTOBER 1, 1922 ❧
NEW YORK CITY, NEW YORK

They've been in all the papers.

Famed San Francisco-born dancer Isadora Duncan, 44, and her new husband, famed Russian poet Sergei Esenin, about to turn 27, make the news by arriving here for the American leg of her dance tour.

Isadora left America when she was 20, and has been living, dancing and teaching in Europe. Last year, the Russian government invited her to move to Moscow and open a dance school.

Last fall, at the studio of a mutual friend, she met the handsome young poet Sergei, already a celebrity in his country. Despite the fact that Isadora speaks English, French and German, but no Russian, and he speaks only Russian, they moved in together almost immediately and married in May. For the wedding Isadora managed to alter her passport to cut their age difference in half.

Isadora Duncan

The newlyweds are in the news here for Isadora's return to her native country with her new young husband.

Throughout the tour they have been in the news for violent, drunken fights in restaurants and wrecked hotel rooms.

❧ FALL, 1922 ❧
DUBLIN; LONDON;
NEW YORK CITY, NEW YORK; AND PARIS

In the September issue of the *Dublin Review, "Domini Canis"* declares that *Ulysses*, the recently published novel by James Joyce, 40, Irish writer living in Paris, is:

❝ A fearful travesty on persons, happenings and intimate life of the most morbid and sickening description...spiritually offensive...[a] Cuchulain of the sewer...[an] Ossian of obscenity...[No Catholic] can even afford to be possessed of a copy of this book, for in its reading lies not only the description but the commission of a sin against the Holy Ghost...Doubtless this book was written to make angels weep and to amuse friends, but we are not sure that 'those embattled angels of the Church, Michael's host' will not laugh aloud to see the failure of this frustrated Titan as he revolves and splutters hopelessly under the flood of his own vomit.❞

"Domini Canis," or "Hound of the Lord," is actually Shane Leslie, 37, Irish writer and diplomat.

❧❧❧

A longer version of the same piece appears the following month in London's *Quarterly Review*, under Leslie's real name. Leslie knows that his readership in England is more likely to be Protestant than Catholic, so he changes a few things:

❝ As a whole, the book must remain impossible to read, and undesirable to quote...We shall not be far wrong if we describe Mr. Joyce's work as literary Bolshevism. It is experimental, anti-Christian, chaotic, totally unmoral...From any Christian point of view this book must be proclaimed anathema, simply because it tries to pour ridicule on the most sacred themes and characters in what had been the religion of Europe for nearly two thousand years."

In late October, poet and playwright Alfred Noyes, 42, delivers a talk to the Royal Society of Literature, which appears in the *Sunday Chronicle* under the title, "Rottenness in Literature":

❝ It is simply the foulest book that has ever found its way into print… [In a court of law] it would be pronounced to be a corrupt mass of indescribable degradation…[This is] the extreme case of complete reduction to absurdity of what I have called 'the literary Bolshevism of the Hour.'"

Noyes has been reading Shane Leslie, obviously.

When Leslie's screed in *The Quarterly Review* is brought to the attention of the Home Office by a concerned citizen, the undersecretary instructs his department to confiscate any copies of *Ulysses* entering the country. Of course, he doesn't have a copy to read himself.

✻❦✻

In New York City, Edmund Wilson, 27, managing editor of *Vanity Fair*, has been quite impressed by *Ulysses* and said so in his review in the July issue of the *New Republic*. He is even more impressed that, as a reward for his insight, he has received a thank you note from Joyce, written by his publisher, American bookshop owner Sylvia Beach, 35.

Postcard from Sylvia Beach

This will make his literary friends green with envy.

❧❧

In Paris, Joyce wants to let his partner, Nora Barnacle, 38, mother of their two children, know how important her support is to him. He gifts her copy number 1000 of *Ulysses*, with a personal inscription, and gives it to her at a dinner party. Nora says she can probably sell it.

❧ EARLY OCTOBER, 1922 ❧

42 RUE FONTAINE, PIGALLE DISTRICT, PARIS; AND THE RESI, PASEO DE LA CASTELLANA, MADRID

At first, it all seemed so interesting.

Writer Andre Breton, 26, was fascinated by the seances he was introduced to by his friend, poet Rene Crevel, 22.

Crevel had passed out during a séance he took part in when on holiday in Normandy last month. After he told Breton and his wife, Simone, 25, about his experience they were eager to try it themselves and enlisted another young poet Robert Desnos, 22, in their activities.

Here at the Bretons' fourth floor apartment, the walls covered with paintings and objects by their friends—Frances Picabia, 43, Pablo Picasso, 40, **Man Ray**, 32—small groups of artists and writers get together almost every evening to play games and practice artistic experiments, such as automatic writing. When their married hosts retire to bed, poet Louis Aragon, just turned 25, and others stay up late and hit the local bars.

But now these nightly seances are getting a bit out of hand. The young poets keep fighting, accusing each other of faking their trances, mostly to get Breton's attention. The neighbors complained about the noise so much, Simone had to bribe the concierge to avoid eviction. Desnos claims he can commune with their friend, painter Marcel Duchamp, 35, in New York City; Crevel says he can predict the future. He predicted that some of the others would get sick—and they did. Picabia and Aragon have decided to stay away.

At another apartment one night, 10 participants go into a trance and try to hang themselves.

Breton figures, enough. He'll get a good article out of this for the magazine he re-launched earlier this year, *Litterature*, and then he'll take off with Simone for a holiday in Spain.

⚜

Near Madrid, about 20 minutes by tram from city centre, at the Residencia de Estudiantes—commonly known as "the Resi"—young male students from the San Fernando Royal Academy of Fine Arts who live here walk around in British-style suits with short, trim, haircuts.

Except one.

First year art student Salvador Dali, 18, from Figueres, Catalonia, skinny and five foot seven, walks around in early 19th century English knee breeches, a long velvet coat to his knees and floppy neckties, sporting a wide-brimmed hat and a gilded cane.

Salvador Dali surrounded by his college friends

Despite his unconventional appearance, Dali is accepted into the conversation groups of the clique known as the Ultra. They publish a student magazine of the same name.

Dali has made particular friends with one of the group members, Luis Bunuel, 22, from Aragon, who has been at the Academy for five years now. Luis has bounced around to different universities, taking up various fields of study—Engineering, Agriculture—but is enjoying his time here, wandering the city streets at night and visiting brothels.

Dali on the other hand has religiously been spending his Sunday mornings in the Prado museum, where he uses pencil and paper to sketch and analyse the works of the great masters.

His new friends in the Ultra gossip all the time about another of their number, writer Frederico Garcia Lorca, 24, who is away this semester but will be returning in January.

Bunuel tells Dali that he will definitely be impressed by Lorca and learn a lot from him. And that he definitely should re-think those clothes.

❧ OCTOBER 11, 1922 ❧
LIBRAIRIE 6, 5 AVENUE DE LOWENDAL;
HOTEL VERNEUIL, RUE DE VERNEUIL, PARIS; AND
74 GLOUCESTER PLACE, MARYLEBONE, LONDON

Sitting in the backroom of Librairie 6, his friend's bookstore and art gallery, English poet and publisher John Rodker, 27, is pretty sure he has everything organized for the big day tomorrow.

In a little more than a month he has managed to pull together the publication of a second edition of the scandalous novel *Ulysses* by Irish-expat in Paris James Joyce, 40, the day before the copies arrive from the Dijon-based printer Darantiere.

Back in England, Rodker had been approached by one of Joyce's many benefactors, Harriet Shaw Weaver, 46, publisher of Joyce through her Egoist Press and *Egoist* magazine.

Weaver has bought the British rights to all Joyce's work, and she is eager to follow up the debut of *Ulysses* this past February, published by the Paris-based bookshop Shakespeare and Company, owned by American ex-pat Sylvia Beach, 35, with a second edition.

John Rodker and his literary friends

Ulysses has been banned in America and confiscated in the UK, so Harriet has determined that the best approach is to have all the production, promotion and administrative work done in Paris, and then ship the books out to other, less tolerant, countries.

Rodker is a good choice for this assignment as he has already founded Ovid Press to publish limited editions, and, as a Conscientious Objector during the Great War, is willing to take risks for his principles.

Joyce, Beach and Weaver look at this second edition as an opportunity to correct the more than 200 typographical errors they've found in Shakespeare and Company's 700-page original. However, rumors are circulating that pirates in the States are hurrying to bring out unauthorized editions. Weaver knows she has to work faster than originally planned. So—no corrections.

From this backroom office Rodker has mailed out flyers trumpeting the publication and then processed the orders. The plan he and Weaver concocted to service the U.S. customers involves him sending a bulk shipment to a collaborative wholesaler in London who will unbind them, pull them apart, shove sections inside British newspapers to avoid confiscation and tariffs, and then send them to the States via a merchant ship with a first mate who has agreed to serve as their smuggler. The American wholesalers will put each clandestine copy back together and deliver it to middlemen and booksellers.

Weaver will finance the whole operation, including £200 for Rodker's services.

Rodker's next step is to receive the shipment of 2,000 copies—complete with typos—from Darantiere tomorrow.

About a half hour's walk across the Left Bank, in the basement of the Hotel Verneuil, Rodker's partner in crime, critic Iris Barry, 27 (actually Sylvia Crump from Birmingham, UK), has set up shop to handle the fulfillment function for individual orders.

In this small room she has gathered rolls of brown parcel paper, piles of mailing labels, scissors and string. When the books arrive tomorrow, she will wrap and tie up each one individually, write out the address of the brave person in America who has ordered it, and then take *Ulysses* to the nearby post office in groups of four or five and send them off with a prayer that each will be delivered to its buyer before U. S. Customs starts confiscating them.

In London, Miss Weaver has decided to handle the delivery to local individuals and bookstores herself. Those copies will be sent by Rodker to a private mailing firm. When the Egoist Press receives an order from a bookshop, Harriet plans to pick up the copies from the mailing company and take them—discreetly—to the store which placed the order. There they will keep *Ulysses* behind the counter until a special customer requests a copy.

Although Weaver's lawyers have advised against it, she is going to keep some copies of *Ulysses* in her office and her home. Her wealthy family has always supported Harriet's work for liberal causes but cannot imagine why she is interested in publishing smut. Her brother-in-law laments,

66 How could she? How could she? An enigma! An enigma!"

❧ OCTOBER 13, 1922

NEW YORK TIMES, NEW YORK CITY, NEW YORK

Publisher Thomas Selzer, Inc., takes an ad in the *New York Times* to announce that three of its latest books are indeed legal.

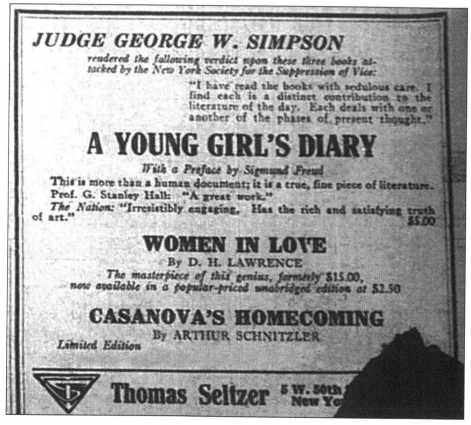

New York Times *advertisement*

❧ MID-OCTOBER, 1922 ❧
THE CRITERION MAGAZINE, LONDON; AND
THE DIAL MAGAZINE, NEW YORK CITY, NEW YORK

"April is the cruelest month..."

Poet, publisher and bank clerk Thomas Stearns Eliot, just turned 34, is proud of this first issue of the magazine he has started, *The Criterion*. His wife, Vivien, also 34, suggested the title. She likes the sound of it.

The production value is good—small format, quality paper, clean typefaces. The contents rises to the standard Eliot set for himself: Longer pieces by top writers from different countries, paid at the rate of £10 for 5,000 words. And no illustrations. He didn't want to junk each issue up the way *The Dial* magazine in the States does, with reproductions of Chagalls and Brancusis spread throughout.

"I will show you fear in a handful of dust..."

Eliot's one disappointment is that he didn't get any work from French writer Marcel Proust, 51, for this first issue, despite interventions by their mutual friend, English novelist Sydney Schiff, 54. However, he is hopeful Proust will submit something in time for Issue No. 2.

Schiff is the first one to congratulate Eliot, who receives his letter while he is looking over the first six copies that have been delivered to him at home.

Praising Eliot's accomplishment in producing *The Criterion*, Schiff also congratulates him on the crown jewel of this issue, Eliot's own epic poem, "The Waste Land," which he has been working on concurrently for the past year or more.

In producing the magazine, Eliot has had the support of Lady Rothermere, 48, who has financed the whole operation with her access to the fortune of her husband, owner of *The Daily Mirror* and *The Daily Mail*. She has even offered Tom an annual £600 stipend and salary for the next three years, but Eliot is concerned that his bosses at the bank won't like the idea of him being on someone else's payroll too.

"A crowd flowed over London Bridge, so many,

I had not thought death had undone so many…"

In writing the poem, Eliot has had the support of many of his literary friends, but none more so than fellow American ex-pat, Ezra Pound, about to turn 37. They met up in Paris early this year and again in Verona at the beginning of summer to "put it through the sieve" as Eliot describes their editing process. The cuts Ezra made were invaluable and Eliot enjoyed collaborating; both agree that the final result is Eliot's best work. Which is why the poem is dedicated to Ezra.

"Those are pearls that were his eyes…"

Now that "The Waste Land" and *The Criterion* have both been loosed upon the United Kingdom, the next step is for the poem to be published in the United States, in the November issue of *The Dial*, on the newsstands in a few days.

After this last year of writing, editing, publishing, negotiating, and taking care of his sick wife—while holding down a full-time job—Eliot is eagerly awaiting the world's reactions to his efforts.

"HURRY UP PLEASE IT'S TIME

Goonight Bill. Goonight Lou. Goonight May. Goonight.

Ta ta. Goonight. Goonight.

Good night, ladies, good night, sweet ladies, good night, good night…"

Pound, in his continuing efforts to get Eliot enough income so that he can afford to leave his bank job, has also been invaluable in getting *The Dial* publisher, Scofield Thayer, 32, to agree to publish "The Waste Land" at all.

At first Thayer offered Eliot $150, based on the magazine's usual payment for poetry, with a little extra thrown in. Eliot wasn't happy with this and prevailed upon another American who had helped with these things before— lawyer and patron of the arts, John Quinn, 52, who had negotiated the deal for the American publication of Eliot's collection, *Poems*, a few years before.

"By the waters of Leman I sat down and wept…"

This time Quinn got Thayer of *The Dial* to agree with Horace Liveright, 37, of Boni and Liveright that "The Waste Land,"
in America, would appear in the November issue of *The Dial* and then be published the following month in book form by Boni and Liveright, with an extended series of notes which Eliot has added.

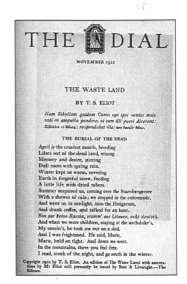

The Dial, *November*

Thayer doesn't like the poem. Or Eliot, for that matter. But his managing editor, Gilbert Seldes, 29, is impressed with "The Waste Land" and, against Thayer's wishes, has made it the main item in the November issue. Seldes is short on copy for the fall issues, so 450 lines of new Eliot is a godsend.

To make sure "The Waste Land" publication has maximum impact, Seldes has enlisted the services of one of the top publicists in the city Bea Kaufman, 27, wife of playwright **George Kaufman**, 32. Seldes enticed her with an invitation for a free meal:

> I want to talk about publicity for T. S. Eliot with you very shortly, and I think that these lofty business matters are always settled at lunch, paid for by the office. Let us go to Child's some morning or afternoon."

In addition to arranging for reviews to appear in the *New York Tribune* and the *New Republic*, and writing one himself for *The Nation*, Seldes also sent an early copy of "The Waste Land" to *Vanity Fair* managing editor Edmund Wilson, 27, asking him to write a review for the December issue of *The Dial*. Wilson read the poem over and over, sitting on the top deck of a Fifth Avenue bus. He feels Eliot's words speak to him as a frustrated writer, living in a crappy apartment that smells like damp cats.

"As a silk hat on a Bradford millionaire..."

No other American magazine or book publisher has been actively involved in bidding for "The Waste Land," but a strong last-minute effort from Quinn was what got Thayer and Liveright to agree to the schedule. Eliot is receiving only $150 from *The Dial*, but they have also agreed to award him their $2,000 Dial Prize this year. (Shhhh—that won't be announced until the December issue.)

As a reward for his pro bono work. Eliot is sending Quinn the original manuscript of "The Waste Land" to add to his collection of authors' manuscripts.

"On Margate Sands.

I can connect

Nothing with nothing..."

Thayer still isn't happy about the poem itself, or its first place position in his magazine. He'd still rather be publishing something from an established novelist like Edith Wharton, 60.

All there is to do now is wait to see what the reviewers and the reading public think.

"Shantih shantih shantih."

❧ LATE OCTOBER, 1922 ❧
UNITED KINGDOM

The most anticipated event in the world of British literature is capturing the attention of poetry lovers across the country: Publication of *Last Poems* by A. E. Housman, 63, the sequel to his previous hit, 26 years ago, *A Shropshire Lad.*

The entire 4,000-copy print run has all been pre-sold, and bookstores in Cambridge sell out their inventory by noon on publication day.

A. E. Housman

❦ OCTOBER 18, 1922 ❧
GRAUMAN'S EGYPTIAN THEATRE,
6706 HOLLYWOOD BOULEVARD,
HOLLYWOOD, CALIFORNIA

❦❧

After more than a year of research, negotiating, planning, hiring, and fund-raising by its star and producer Douglas Fairbanks, 39,

After more than $1.4 million of the producer's own money,

After more than 500 workers behind the scenes,

After thousands of extras, mostly highly trained, unemployed veterans from the Great War,

After thousands of historically accurate costumes, shields and lances,

The Set

The Cast

After thousands of looks of amazement on the faces
of tourists coming to gawk at the movie set at
Santa Monica Boulevard and La Brea,

Produced by Douglas Fairbanks Pictures Corporation
and distributed by United Artists,

For the price of $5 a ticket,

Starring Douglas Fairbanks, Wallace Beery
and Alan Hale, Sr.,

Douglas Fairbanks in

Robin Hood

premieres at the opening of

Grauman's Egyptian Theatre,

The first time any Hollywood feature has ever
been premiered in Hollywood, California.

❧ OCTOBER 21, 1922 ❧
82 MERRION SQUARE, DUBLIN

Poet, playwright, and Abbey Theatre co-founder **William Butler Yeats**, 57, writes to a friend from his new family home:

❝ I think what I say of Ireland, at least, may interest you. I think things are coming right [for the new country] slowly but very slowly; we have had years now of murder and arson in which both nations have shared impartially. In my own neighborhood [of Thoor Ballylee, in the west of Ireland] the Black and Tans dragged two young men tied alive to a lorry by their heels, till their bodies were rent in pieces.

'There was nothing for the mother but the head' said a countryman and the head he spoke of was found on the road side. The one enlivening Truth that starts out of it all is that we may learn charity after mutual contempt. There is a no longer a virtuous nation and the best of us live by candlelight…

I am working at present at the project of getting the Abbey Theatre adopted as the Irish State Theatre and I think I may succeed."

The author with the Abbey Theatre logo at the Abbey pub in Boston, Massachusetts

❧ LATE OCTOBER, 1922 ❧
LA PRIEURE, AVON, NEAR
CHATEAU FOUNTAINEBLEAU, FRANCE

When she wakes up each morning, the first thing New Zealand-born writer Katherine Mansfield, just turned 34, smells is cow manure.

When she arrived at this commune a few weeks ago, the founder and guru, Georgi Gurdjieff, maybe 50, examined her and determined that she shouldn't be required to take part in the manual labor that his other disciples carry out—butchering pigs, building huge structures on the grounds.

But Gurdjieff is requiring Mansfield to sleep on this platform directly above the cows in the barn because, he says, it will cure her tuberculosis.

Mansfield is not so sure. But she does feel that practicing regular discipline, helping out in the kitchen by peeling vegetables, taking cold baths, making her own bed—even if it is in the barn—has so far been beneficial to her. Although she keeps her fur coat on all the time against the cold, she feels that this regimen is more helpful than the quack doctors she consulted in Paris earlier in the year.

Gurdjieff established his Institute for the Harmonious Development of Man here in this crumbling monastery at the beginning of the month. He claims he has been able to fund it with the fees he has earned from treating wealthy addicts, from speculation in commodity markets, and from a few restaurants he operates in Montmartre. But word is that he has also received money from Lady Rothermere, 48, wife of the owner of *The Daily Mirror* and *The Daily Express* in London. The Brits turned Gurdjieff down for citizenship, so he figures he'll just take their money instead.

Since coming here, Mansfield hasn't been in touch often with her husband, former editor of *The Athenaeum* John Middleton Murry, 33, and friends, like novelist **Virginia Woolf**, 40, back in England. She doesn't interact much with Gurdjieff's fellow Russian refugees who have followed him here either. Her closest companions are her old friend and mentor, Alfred Richard Orage, 49, who gave up the editorship of *The New Age* magazine to come live here, and her new friend and assigned handler, Olga Lazovic, 23.

Most of Gurdjieff's 100 disciples gladly sleep in uncomfortable cottages or unheated rooms in the main building which they work hard at restoring all day. Known as "The Ritz," that's where the good rooms are, reserved for Gurdjieff and his celebrity guests.

Georgi Gurdjieff

Katherine does take part in the dances, games and rituals, many including vodka, which Gurdjieff imposes on them all. One of his favorites is "Stop." They all move around until he yells, "Stop!" From the throne he sits on. And they stop.

Mansfield is hopeful that, of all the "cures" she has tried, this one will actually work.

❧ OCTOBER 27, 1922 ❧
HOGARTH HOUSE, RICHMOND, LONDON

The Hogarth Press, founded and operated by **Virginia Woolf**, 40, and her husband **Leonard**, 41, has just published its first full-length work, 290 pages, 60,000 words, **Virginia's** third novel *Jacob's Room*.

In its past five years, the Press has successfully produced and marketed collections of short stories and smaller works. Until now, Virginia's novels have been published by her stepbrother, Gerald Duckworth, 51, so they had to get his permission to break the contract. Good riddance.

With a cover by **Virginia's** sister, painter **Vanessa Bell**, 43, the Woolfs are pleased with the finished product. **Virginia's** American publisher, Donald Brace, 40, is eager to bring it out there, telling **Virginia** how much he admires her work. This has at least made her feel, as she writes in her diary, that the novel "cannot be wholly frigid fireworks."

Advance copies have been sent to their Bloomsbury friends, who tell her it is her best work. Essayist **Lytton Strachey**, 42, is the first to mention the main character's similarities to **Virginia** and **Vanessa's** brother, Thoby Stephen, who died 16 years ago from typhoid at the age of 26. **Lytton** writes to **Virginia**,

❝ How you manage to leave out everything that's dreary, and yet retain enough string for your pearls I can hardly understand."

Virginia is thinking sales might hit 800 copies by June. When they get to 650 they'll order a second edition. About 30 of the thousand or so they've printed have sold before publication day, today.

The **Woolfs** are counting on the success of *Jacob's Room* to help their fledgling publishing company. They've hung on so far, but they feel as though **Leonard's** assistant, Ralph Partridge, 28, is holding them back. He and **Leonard** fight constantly, and Ralph has screwed up some of the promotion for previous books. They've met a few young people recently who might be better at the role but haven't chucked Partridge out yet.

They're hoping for good reviews in major publications. **Virginia** is most concerned about *The Times Literary Supplement*, as she writes in her diary,

❝ Not that it will be the most intelligent, but it will be the most read & I can't bear people to see me downed in public."

✂❀✂

Virginia has already begun her next novel, concurrently with writing essays to be published as *The Common Reader*. She noted a few weeks ago that her short story, "Mrs. Dalloway in Bond Street," has "branched into a book." She hasn't decided on a title yet, but she is working out passages and making detailed notes in a journal labeled, "Book of scraps of J's R. & first version of The Hours," some in brief lines down the side of the page.

completely separately...some sort of fusion..."The Prime Minister"...must converge upon the party at the end... ushers in a host of others...much in relief...interludes of thought, or reflection, or short digressions...related, logically, to the rest?...all compact, yet not jerked...At Home: or The Party...the 10th of June or whatever I call it...& I adumbrate here a study of insanity & suicide: the world seen by the sane & the insane side by side—something like that...Septimus Smith? is that a good name...a possible revision of this book: Suppose it to be connected in this way:

Sanity and insanity.

Mrs. D. seeing the truth. S. S. seeing the insane truth...

The contrast must be arranged...

The pace is to be given by the gradual increase of S's Insanity. On the one side, by the approach of the party on the other.

The design is extremely complicated...

All to take place in one day?"

❧ OCTOBER 29, 1922 ❧
THE LITTLE CHURCH AROUND THE CORNER, 1 EAST 29TH STREET, NEW YORK CITY; AND EAST SHORE ROAD, GREAT NECK, LONG ISLAND, NEW YORK

This wedding is fun. The Manhattan editors and writers who trade quips and insults almost every day at lunch at the Algonquin Hotel are here. The groom is Robert Sherwood, 26, editor of the humor magazine *Life*, towering over everyone at six feet eight inches tall. The bride is actress Mary Brandon, 20, who appeared with Sherwood and the Algonquin gang in their one-off revue, *No Sirree!*, a few months ago.

The ushers include Sherwood's co-editor at *Life*, **Robert Benchley**, 33, who just finished a gig with the *Music Box Revue* doing his shtick from *No Sirree!*, "The Treasurer's Report," seven days a week.

And **Alexander Woollcott**, 35, who just went from reviewing plays for the *New York Times* to writing a column, "In the Wake of the Plays," for the *New York Herald* after the owner, Frank Munsey, 68, offered him $15,000 a year. "For money and no other reason," explains **Woollcott**.

And playwright **Marc Connelly**, 31, who just had a second Broadway hit, *West of Pittsburgh*, with his collaborator, **George S Kaufman**, 32.

And also Frank Case, 49, who is not known to be particularly witty, but as the manager of the Algonquin Hotel, he must have a good sense of humor.

Also attending are hit novelist **F. Scott Fitzgerald**, 26, and his wife Zelda, 22, fresh off the successful publication of his second collection of short stories, *Tales of the Jazz Age*.

And America's sweethearts, film stars Mary Pickford, 30, and her co-star and husband of two years, Douglas Fairbanks, 39.

All wish the Sherwoods well. But some predict this wedding will be the high point of their marriage.

❧❧❧

Many of the wedding guests actually have more fun in the summer and into the fall partying out on Long Island.

Herbert Bayard Swope's house in Great Neck

The biggest bashes are at the rented home of *New York World* publisher Herbert Bayard Swope, 40, overlooking Manhasset Bay. People were not invited—they went there.

From Great Neck then, came the **Fitzgeralds**, who have rented a house there and the Lardners from across the street. And a whole clan named Marx, including Arthur ("Harpo"), 33, and his brother Julius ("Groucho"), 32, who have made a name for themselves in musical theatre.

From nearby Sandy Point came magazine illustrator Neysa McMein, 34, and mining engineer Jack Baragwanath, 35. Neysa was the first to suggest that their competitive croquet games on the lawn be played without rules. Swope loved the idea; he feels the game

 makes you want to cheat and kill...The game gives release to all the evil in you."

Heywood Broun, 33, a columnist on Swope's own *World*, came to gamble, but sometimes brought his wife, free-lance writer Ruth Hale, 35.

Of theatrical people there were the **Kaufmans** and **Connelly** and composer George Gershwin, 24. Also from New York were **Woollcott**, and *New York Times* journalist Jane Grant, 30. And the free-lance writer **Dorothy Parker**, 29, separated now, who has pieces in almost every issue of the *Saturday Evening Post*. She's sometimes accompanied by her latest beau, would-be playwright Charles MacArthur, 27, but other times is seen sneaking across the road to the home of sportswriter Ring Lardner, 37, when his wife is away.

In addition to all these, satiric writer Donald Ogden Stewart, 27, came there at least once.

All these people came to Swope's house in the summer.

❧ END OF OCTOBER, 1922 ❧
ITALY; GERMANY; AND IRELAND

In Rome, National Fascist Party leader Benito Mussolini, 39, wearing a black shirt and trousers and a bowler hat, arrives to form a government and become the youngest Prime Minister in Italy's history, at the request of King Victor Emmanuel III, 52.

In Florence, American ex-pat art historian Bernard Berenson, 57, tells a visiting friend,

> 66 These Fascists are the same people who requisitioned my most precious wines three years ago in the name of the Florentine Soviet Committee; then they were Communists. They don't know what they are. The only lucky Italians are the ones who live abroad. I've lived here for 32 years and I've never seen a government and that's their way of governing, like their police, who lie low during strikes. When the government comes up against some difficulty they disappear; when everything

Benito Mussolini leading the March on Rome

is settled by the nature of things, they reappear, triumphant. But nevertheless everything works in this country. That's because Italy isn't a nation; it's a civilization."

❧❧❧

In Berlin, journalist Count Harry Kessler, 54, president of the German Peace Society, writes in his diary,

❝   Perhaps [Mussolini] will usher in a period of fresh European disorders and wars…This may turn out to be a black day for Italy and Europe."

In Dublin, poet and playwright **William Butler Yeats**, 57, admires Mussolini's "burst of powerful personality."

❧ FIRST WEEK IN NOVEMBER ❧
HOGARTH HOUSE, RICHMOND, LONDON

The **Woolfs** are looking ahead to their upcoming weekend in the country with mixed feelings.

Virginia, 40, and **Leonard**, 41, who operate the Hogarth Press here, will be spending a couple of days at the Mill House, Tidmarsh, in Berkshire with three of their friends who live there together, essayist **Lytton Strachey**, 42; painter Dora Carrington, 29; and

Dora Carrington, Ralph Partridge and Lytton Strachey

Ralph Partridge, 28, who has been the Hogarth Press assistant for the past year or so.

Carrington moved to Tidmarsh with **Lytton** about five years ago, knowing full well that he is homosexual; Partridge moved in after he met Carrington through her brother at Oxford. Last year, **Strachey** paid for their wedding and joined them on their honeymoon. The threesome rents the house from another Bloomsbury friend, economist **John Maynard Keynes**, 39.

Both **Virginia** and **Leonard** are protective of their home-based business, Hogarth Press, and this has led to many fights between **Leonard** and Ralph. But Ralph has refused to leave.

In many of her diary entries **Virginia** has referred to Ralph as "lazy, undependable, now industrious, now slack, unadventurous, all corroded by **Lytton**, can't praise, yet has no view of his own," and has questioned his "lumpiness, grumpiness, slovenliness, & stupidity versus his niceness, strength, fundamental amiability & connections."

Recently, the **Woolfs** have been introduced to some young people who might be suitable additions, but Ralph was furious when they offered a job share to one woman.

In the past few weeks, they have been talking to a young American who was interested in managing the Press for them, but they think he'll try to turn their publishing house, which is focused on turning out quality content, into a precious press that is more concerned with fancy paper and bindings. Fortunately, the young man has decided that the commute would be too onerous. **Virginia** didn't want to hire an American anyway.

They're hoping to discuss Partridge's future this weekend with **Lytton**, who has hinted that he will no longer have Hogarth as his publisher if they get rid of Ralph. **Virginia** and **Leonard** are thinking that might not be a bad trade off.

❧ NOVEMBER 6, 1922 ❧
VALLEY OF THE KINGS, EGYPT

Two days ago, Howard Carter, 48, and his team of British archaeologists uncovered a stone step.

Yesterday, they cleared it off and found an entrance.

Today, Carter sends a telegram to his patron, George Edward Stanhope Molyneux Herbert, the fifth Earl of Carnarvon, 56, at his family home, Highclere Castle, in Newbury:

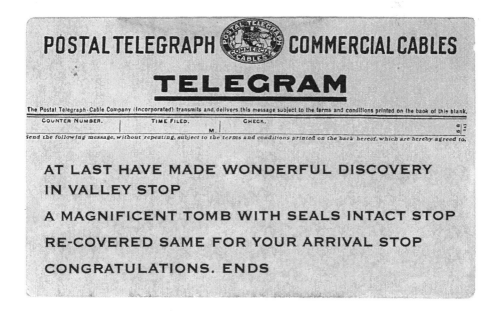

POSTAL TELEGRAPH COMMERCIAL CABLES

TELEGRAM

The Postal Telegraph-Cable Company (Incorporated) transmits and delivers this message subject to the terms and conditions printed on the back of this blank.

COUNTER NUMBER.	TIME FILED.	CHECK.

Send the following message, without repeating, subject to the terms and conditions printed on the back hereof, which are hereby agreed to.

AT LAST HAVE MADE WONDERFUL DISCOVERY IN VALLEY STOP

A MAGNIFICENT TOMB WITH SEALS INTACT STOP

RE-COVERED SAME FOR YOUR ARRIVAL STOP

CONGRATULATIONS. ENDS

❧ EARLY NOVEMBER, 1922 ❧
PENSION NOWE, RONDA SAN PEDRO,
BARCELONA, SPAIN

Had he not promised to give the lecture, French writer Andre Breton, 26, and his wife Simone, 25, would head back to Paris today.

But they drove here with their friends, painter Francis Picabia, 43, and his mistress, for the opening of an exhibit of Picabia's work at the Dalmau Gallery, and Breton promised to deliver a lecture about the current state of art in France.

It took over a week to get here, in Picabia's sporty Mercer convertible. Breton wore his leather pilot's helmet, goggles and his heavy fur coat. In Marseilles they stopped to see a disappointing exhibit with fake African artefacts, where Breton spent 20 francs on a stuffed armadillo. Which woke up and jumped out of his arms.

Since they arrived in Barcelona, Simone has been bedridden with salmonella poisoning. The only saving grace has been the Gaudi architecture throughout the town. Andre sent a postcard of the cathedral Sagrada Familia to his Spanish friend back in Paris, painter Pablo Picasso, 41, asking,

❝ Do you know this marvel?"

In his talk Breton is planning to announce, in French to an audience of Spaniards, his belief that the Dada movement is over. He feels that there is a new movement brewing, which involves artists such as Picabia, Picasso, and American **Man Ray**, 32, but they are so far unorganized and un-named.

❧ MID-NOVEMBER, 1922 ❧
DEL MONTE RANCH, NEAR TAOS, NEW MEXICO

Enough was enough. English novelist David Herbert Lawrence, 37, and his German wife Frieda, 43, are definitely grateful to their hostess, American patron of the arts Mabel Dodge, 43, who invited them to come live here so David can write about the local area.

But after about two months, living next door to the formidable Mabel has proved too much. She monopolizes David's time which angers Frieda.

And why has she partnered with this Native American, Tony Luhan, 43. Lawrence thinks Tony has just fallen for Mabel's money.

So David and Frieda have found this ranch far enough up the mountain to be out of Mabel's grasp, but close enough to be polite. A bit less comfortable physically, but worth it to have their freedom.

The owner of this compound supports artists as well—there are two young Danish painters living in another building—but in a more hands-off manner than Dodge.

David and Frieda are enjoying horseback riding in cowboy hats and boots, but in general find the area depressing.

Shortly after they arrived, Lawrence had written to his friend back in England, novelist E. M. Forster, 43,

Entrance to Mabel Dodge's house

    ❝   Taos is a tiny place 30 miles from the railway high up—6,000 ft.—in the desert. I feel a great stranger, but have got used to that feeling, & prefer it to feeling 'homely.' After all, one is a stranger, nowhere so hopelessly as at home."

❧ NOVEMBER 15, 1922 ❧
UNITED KINGDOM

The results are in.

National:

Conservatives, 344 seats; party leader Bonar Law, 64, becomes Prime Minister.

Labour, 142 seats; doubling the number they held before, Labour becomes the main opposition party for the first time.

Liberals, 112 seats; split between its two branches, Liberals and National Liberals.

Selected constituencies:

Dundee, Scotland, two seats: Winners are Labour and, for the first time in any election, Scottish Prohibition; two National Liberal candidates, including incumbent Winston Churchill, about to turn 48, come in third and fourth.

Combined English Universities, two seats: Winners are Unionist and National Liberal, H. A. L. Fisher, 57, incumbent and cousin of novelist **Virginia Woolf**, 40; an Independent and Labour, **Leonard Woolf**, about to turn 42, husband of **Virginia Woolf**, come in third and fourth.

❧❦❧

Yesterday, the British Broadcasting Company began operating out of Marconi House in the Strand, over London station, 2LO.

Today, the BBC has already expanded its reach by opening stations in Birmingham and Manchester.

❧ MID-NOVEMBER, 1922 ❧
MIDTOWN MANHATTAN, NEW YORK CITY, NEW YORK

At the Sam H. Harris Theatre on West 42nd Street, *Hamlet*, starring the legendary John Barrymore, 40, has just opened. *The New York Herald* says that his performance "will be memorable in the history of the American theatre."

The *Times* predicts,

❝ We have a new and a lasting Hamlet."

And *Brooklyn Life* says that Barrymore has "won the right to be called the greatest living American tragedian."

❧❧❧

Farther up Fifth Avenue, the Cort Theatre on 48th Street is hosting a different type of theatrical success, *Merton of the Movies*, by Algonquin Hotel lunch buddies **Marc Connelly**, 31, and **George S Kaufman**, just turning 33. Like their previous Broadway hit *Dulcy*, *Merton* is based on a suggestion from another regular at the Algonquin, top *World* columnist **Franklin Pierce Adams**, just turning 41, known to all as **FPA**.

The *Times* calls it "a delight in every way," and their other lunch regular, **Heywood Broun**, 33, also in the *World*, calls it "the most amusing show of the season."

❧❧❧

But, around the corner at the much smaller Punch and Judy Theatre on 49th Street, **Connelly** and **Kaufman** have financed a comedy review, *The '49ers*, written by their friends.

May Irwin

The gang put on a show back in April, *No Sirree!*, which was only performed one night for an invited audience of their friends and fans, who loved it.

So they figured they'd do it right this time—hire a producer, director and professional actors. Besides **Connelly**, **Kaufman**, **FPA** and **Broun**, the sketches were written by their talented friends, including **Dorothy Parker**, 29, **Robert Benchley**, 33, and Ring Lardner, 37.

What could go wrong?!

It wasn't funny.

On opening night, the Mistress of Ceremonies, legendary vaudevillian Miss May Irwin, 60, was soooo bad, **Connelly** decided to take on the role himself, over **Kaufman's** objections.

The whole disaster just closed after only 15 performances.

※⌘※

One block away, at Tony Soma's speakeasy, **Parker** is sharing the horror story of her recent abortion with anyone who will listen. Few want to.

She'd felt sick when her friend, magazine illustrator Neysa McMein, 34, was painting her portrait recently. Neysa gave her a glass of gin and immediately got her to a west side hospital.

They both knew who the father was: That cad, would-be playwright Charles MacArthur, 27.

When **Dotty** told Charlie that she had had an abortion, he slipped her 30 bucks, which did not cover the cost, and promptly disappeared from her life.

Parker said,

❝ It was like Judas making a refund."

To make it worse, due to her sloppy timekeeping, **Parker** had passed her first trimester, and "Dr. Sunshine" (one of many so-called in Manhattan) was angry that her pregnancy was farther along than she had claimed.

After one week in the hospital, **Parker** is back to her usual writing, reviewing and drinking. She has poems regularly in the *Saturday Evening Post*, and her first short story, "Such a Pretty Little Picture" will be in next month's *Smart Set*.

But this whole experience has truly depressed her. Her pal **Benchley** is supportive, but he warned her about MacArthur, who has become one of **Benchley's** best friends.

She tells him,

❝ Serves me right for putting all my eggs in one bastard."

❧ NOVEMBER 20, 1922 ❧
UNION HOTEL ETOILE, 44 RUE HAMELIN, PARIS

American ex-pat photographer **Man Ray**, 32, has been called here, along with two painters and a sculptor, to record the corpse of French writer Marcel Proust, 51, who died two days ago.

Ray has made a bit of a name for himself in Paris this past year, and this month's *Vanity Fair* magazine has four of his "rayographs," a new technique he has been working on.

Proust had been complaining to his friends that he was ill for months but didn't feel as though they took him seriously. He told his loyal housekeeper Celeste Albaret, 31, that she must keep the doctors away from him in his last hours, to let the natural process unfold—or he will come back to haunt her.

Proust had been fighting the recommendations of his doctors, including his brother Robert, 49, for months while he experienced increasing fame and sales of his books, along with increasing health issues.

In the spring he took an accidental overdose of his adrenalin and was left screaming in pain. After that his chauffeur, Celeste's husband, had to bring Proust daily chilled beer and ice cream from the Ritz Hotel.

In the summer, he had a big night out on the town with French writer Jean Cocteau, 33, at their favorite nightclub, Le Boeuf sur la toit, but that ended in a brawl and Proust challenging his young attacker to a duel the next morning. The kid apologized.

This fall Proust had violent fits of asthma and vertigo which caused him to fall whenever he got out of bed. He blamed carbon monoxide from the fireplace, and commanded Celeste to stop lighting the fire. So he was surrounded by cold.

The doctors told Proust not to go out; Proust went for a walk, started sneezing and came home.

The doctors told him to eat a lot and rest; instead he followed his mother's instructions to him as a child, eating nothing but milk and fruit and throwing himself into writing and rewriting.

At the end Marcel submitted to injections from the doctors, but he grabbed Celeste's wrist and pinched her as hard as he could, telling her she shouldn't have let them come.

At 5:30 in the afternoon he was pronounced dead in this room.

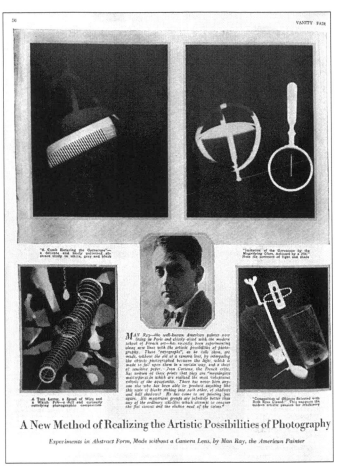

A New Method of Realizing the Artistic Possibilities of Photography

Experiments in Abstract Form, Made without a Camera Lens, by Man Ray, the American Painter

Man Ray *in Vanity Fair*

Now, two days later, about a dozen family and friends have been invited to view the body, and **Ray** to photograph it.

Seeing his friend lying in state, surrounded by his manuscripts, Cocteau notes,

❝ That pile of paper on his left was still alive, like watches ticking on the wrists of dead soldiers."

❧ NOVEMBER 23, 1922 ❧

NEW YORK TIMES, NEW YORK CITY, NEW YORK; AND FOURTH WORLD CONGRESS OF THE COMMUNIST INTERNATIONAL, MOSCOW

In Moscow, Jamaican-American writer Claude McKay, 32, has given his speech to the Fourth World Congress of the Communist International on the topic, "The Negro Question," which was well-received. McKay financed this trip, which he calls his "Magic Pilgrimage," by selling deluxe editions of his poetry collection, *Harlem Shadows*, to people on the donor list of the National Association of Colored People (NAACP) and working as a stoker on a freighter.

Lynching was only made a federal hate crime in the United States in March of 2022 when President Joe Biden signed the Emmett Till Anti-Lynching bill. For more information, click here: https://rollcall. com/2022/03/29/biden-signs-federal-anti-lynching-law/

Ad placed in the New York Times *by the NAACP*

❧ NOVEMBER 26, 1922 ❧
VALLEY OF THE KINGS, EGYPT

When he first received the telegram from English archeologist Howard Carter, 48, about a "wonderful discovery" at the site of a pharaoh's tomb in Egypt's Valley of the Kings, Lord George Herbert, Fifth Earl of Carnarvon, 56, was not overly impressed. In the 13 years Carnarvon has been funding Carter's adventures, the archeologist has often been wrong about how wonderful his discoveries are. Carnarvon cabled back,

> **POSTAL TELEGRAPH   COMMERCIAL CABLES**
>
> **TELEGRAM**
>
> The Postal Telegraph-Cable Company (Incorporated) transmits and delivers this message subject to the terms and conditions printed on the back of this blank.
>
> | COUNTER NUMBER. | TIME FILED. | CHECK. |
> | --- | --- | --- |
>
> Send the following message, without repeating, subject to the terms and conditions printed on the back hereof, which are hereby agreed to.
>
> **POSSIBLY COME SOON**

But the more he thought about it, Carnarvon started to feel as though he should make a point of getting there right away. This is, after all, the tomb of King Tutankhamun, the young pharaoh who reigned in the 14th century BC, dying at the age of 18, after only nine years on the throne.

So he cabled again—

POSTAL TELEGRAPH COMMERCIAL CABLES

TELEGRAM

The Postal Telegraph-Cable Company (Incorporated) transmits and delivers this message subject to the terms and conditions printed on the back of this blank.

COUNTER NUMBER.	TIME FILED.	CHECK.

Send the following message, without repeating, subject to the terms and conditions printed on the back hereof, which are hereby agreed to.

PROPOSE ARRIVE ALEXANDRIA TWENTIETH

—packed up his daughter, Lady Evelyn Herbert, 21, and took off for Luxor.

They arrived here yesterday, and today Carter is taking them to the site. He shows them the stone step his team unearthed a few weeks ago and begins to break through what is clearly the entrance.

As Carter looks through the hole he has made in the vault's sealed door, Carnarvon asks him,

 Can you see anything?"

Carter replies,

 Yes—wonderful things."

❧ NOVEMBER 30, 1922 ☙
9 CLARENCE GATE GARDENS, MARYLEBONE, LONDON

At least he got an apology.

Poet Thomas Stearns Eliot, 34, was livid two weeks ago when he read the *Liverpool Daily Post and Mercury's* "Books and Bookmen" column about his latest poem, "The Waste Land."

Yes, his friends, at the instigation of another American ex-pat poet, Ezra Pound, 37, have formed a fund called *Bel Esprit* with the idea of supporting Eliot's work financially. BUT. He has NOT left his job at Lloyds Bank. His friends did NOT get together in some sort of surprise meeting to tell him about the fund. And, God knows, he NEVER said to them,

> ❝ Thank you all very much; I shall make good use of the money, but I like the bank!"

Pound's efforts to establish *Bel Esprit* have made Eliot uncomfortable. Just yesterday, he wrote to Ezra in Paris, questioning whether this annual stipend would continue for his life, or for the life of his wife, Vivien, 34, too. His friends feel that Vivien, who has been quite ill, is a drain on Tom. But, as he has written to Pound,

Vivien Eliot

> ❝ She kept me from returning to America where I should have become a professor and probably never written another line of poetry."

Some of the hogwash in the newspaper article comes from a piece that Pound published in *New Age* magazine this past March. That was embarrassing enough, with Ezra referring to Tom's "complete physical breakdown." Other specifics in the *Liverpool Daily* piece MUST have been leaked to the writer from one of Eliot's English friends.

No matter the source, Tom has been consulting lawyers to see if he can sue the newspaper. He wrote a forceful letter to the editor denying all the lies and stating,

66   The circulation of untrue stories of this kind causes me profound astonishment and annoyance and may also do me considerable harm."

Today the paper has published his letter, followed by a full apology, signed by the editor.

❧ December 2 and 3, 1922 ❧
Gare de Lyon, Paris; and Lausanne, Switzerland

I t's gone. The valise.

She knows the porter put it right there. And she went to get a bottle of water. She's come back. And now it's gone.

American ex-pat Hadley Hemingway, 31, is traveling to Lausanne, Switzerland, to visit her husband, American foreign correspondent for the *Toronto Star*, **Ernest Hemingway**, 23, who is covering the Lausanne Peace Conference.

Ernie's been there for about a week; he'd begged her to come with him, but Hadley hadn't been feeling well. When she received his letter yesterday saying how much he missed her, she threw together some skiing clothes and stuffed a small valise full of the fiction stories he's been working on. Hadley figured he'd want to show them to his friend, American investigative reporter Lincoln Steffens, 56.

And now they're gone.

She finds the porter who helped her and they search the whole train. Nada.

Hadley is devastated. How is she going to tell **Ernie**?! All his hard work. His first novel. The writing that is so much more important to him than the journalism he's being paid for.

All the carbons were in the valise too.

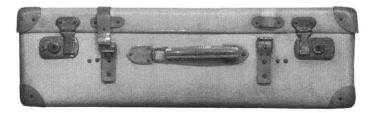

In Lausanne, **Hemingway** is filing story after story about the conference which brings together leaders from Great Britain, France, Greece, Italy and Turkey.

For the *Toronto Star*. But also for the American Hearst publications. And the International News Service (INS), using the name "John Hadley," so the *Star* won't catch him.

But the INS has become suspicious. They have asked for some more details about the expense claims **Hemingway** has been turning in. That just makes **Ernie** angry, so he sends them a cable:

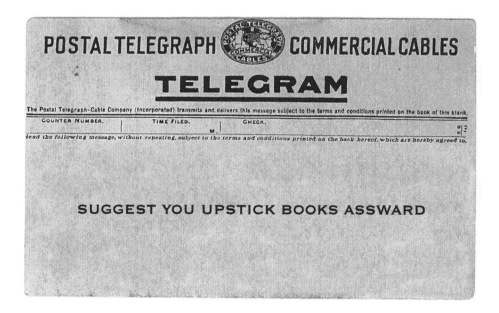

POSTAL TELEGRAPH COMMERCIAL CABLES

TELEGRAM

The Postal Telegraph-Cable Company (Incorporated) transmits and delivers this message subject to the terms and conditions printed on the back of this blank.

COUNTER NUMBER. | TIME FILED. | CHECK.

Send the following message, without repeating, subject to the terms and conditions printed on the back hereof, which are hereby agreed to.

SUGGEST YOU UPSTICK BOOKS ASSWARD

Today **Hemingway** is looking forward to seeing his wife, Hadley, just arriving from Paris. At the train station he sees her step out onto the platform. He can't believe the look on her face. She's obviously been crying for hours. What on earth could have happened to upset her so much?!

董 LATE NOVEMBER INTO 董 DECEMBER, 1922
HOLLYWOOD, CALIFORNIA

A*Woman of Paris*, which is filming here, is the first serious dramatic feature from the world's best known and best loved clown, Charlie Chaplin, 33.

Having just fulfilled his contract with First National Pictures, Chaplin has set up a new film studio, United Artists, with his friends, actors Douglas Fairbanks, 39, and Mary Pickford, 30, and director D. W. Griffith, 47.

Charlie has written it—although he hasn't actually produced a screenplay; he has it all worked out in his head. He cast the major parts—he really wants to give his frequent co-star, Edna Purviance, 27, a chance to shine. He is directing it. All of which he has done before.

But he isn't in it. That's a first.

He wrote himself a little three-second cameo playing an inept porter, but he's not listed in the credits.

Charlie has based the story on tales his recent lover, Mrs. Peggy Hopkins Joyce, 29, former actress, former Ziegfield girl, former wife of three or four millionaires, has told him about her exciting romantic life.

A Woman of Paris is an opportunity for Chaplin to move away from his comedic "Tramp" persona and experiment with the medium of film. His incredibly talented cameraman, Rollie Totheroe, just turning 32, even figured out a way to create the image of an approaching train at night using just lighting. No train.

Charlie is really hoping his fans will like this one as much as they have his other 70 films.

❧ DECEMBER, 1922 ❧
ON THE NEWSSTANDS OF AMERICA

When *Babbitt* by Sinclair Lewis, 37, was published a few months ago, it was met with mostly positive reactions.

H. L. Mencken, 42, literary critic for *Smart Set*, found the main character to be a symbol of everything wrong with American culture:

Babbitt *by Sinclair Lewis*

❝ It is not what [Babbitt] feels and aspires that moves him primarily; it is what the folks about him will think of him. His politics is communal politics, mob politics, herd politics; his religion is a public rite wholly without subjective significance."

Rebecca West, just turned 30, in *The New Statesman*, declared that *Babbitt* "has that something extra, over and above, which makes the work of art."

Fellow novelist H. G. Wells, 56, told Lewis that it is

❝ One of the greatest novels I have read…I wish I could have written *Babbitt*."

Somerset Maugham, 48, wrote to say that he felt that

❝ It is a much better book than *Main Street*."

Edith Wharton, 60, to whom the novel is dedicated, wrote from one of her villas in France,

" I wonder how much of it the American public, to whom irony seems to have become unintelligible as Chinese, will even remotely feel?... Thank you again for associating my name with a book I so warmly admire and applaud."

But now in December, Edmund Wilson, 27, has his say in *Vanity Fair*, comparing Lewis unfavorably to Dickens and Twain, and stating that Lewis' literary gift "is almost entirely for making people nasty."

※※※

Last month *The Dial* published "The Waste Land" by T. S. Eliot, 34, and in this month's issue the publisher, Scofield Thayer, just turned 33, announces that Eliot is the second recipient of the magazine's annual Dial Prize of $2,000.

In the same issue, Eliot has a piece about the death of English vaudeville star, Marie Lloyd, aged 52, which depressed Eliot terribly. In October, almost 100,000 mourners attended her funeral in London.

This issue of *The Dial* also contains Edmund Wilson's praise of "The Waste Land," an in-depth piece about Eliot's importance as a poet:

" He feels intensely and with distinction and speaks naturally in beautiful verse...The race of the poets—though grown rare—is not yet quite dead."

Eliot is pleased with Wilson's review, but unhappy that Wilson called his fellow ex-pat Ezra Pound, 37, an "imitator of [Eliot]...extremely ill-focused." Eliot considers Pound to be the greatest living English-language poet.

※※※

In *The Nation* this month, *Dial* editor Gilbert Seldes, 29, is also enamored of "The Waste Land," comparing it to *Ulysses* by James Joyce, 40, published earlier this year:

> ❝ That 'The Waste Land' is, in a sense, the inversion and the complement of *Ulysses* is at least tenable. We have in *Ulysses* the poet defeated, turning outward, savoring the ugliness which is no longer transmutable into beauty, and, in the end, homeless. We have in 'The Waste Land' some indication of the inner life of such a poet. The contrast between the forms of these two works is not expressed in the recognition that one is among the longest and one among the shortest of works in its genre; the important thing is that in each the theme, once it is comprehended, is seen to have dictated the form."

Eliot sends Seldes a nice note thanking him for the review.

Outlook magazine, on the other hand, features "A Flapper's Appeal to Parents," asking parents and society as a whole to be more understanding of these dancing females who spend "a large amount of time in automobiles."

First described by American novelist **F. Scott Fitzgerald**, 26, the flapper grows up in his story in this month's *Metropolitan* magazine, "Winter Dreams," about a midwestern boy in love with a

Metropolitan, *December*

selfish rich girl, who marries someone all wrong for her. When writing the story, **Fitzgerald** cut some descriptions to save them for his third novel, which he is working on now.

✺❁✺

The December *Smart Set* has the first short story by one of America's most-published and most popular poets, **Dorothy Parker**, 29, whose "Such a Pretty Little Picture" describes a man living a monotonous life in the suburbs, just cutting his hedge. Similar to her best friend, fellow Algonquin Round Table member **Robert Benchley**, 33, who lives in Scarsdale with his wife and two sons.

❧ DECEMBER 15, 1922 ❧
NEW YORK CITY, NEW YORK; AND
9 CLARENCE GATE GARDENS, MARYLEBONE, LONDON

After nearly a year of negotiating, between the publisher, Horace Liveright, just turned 38, in New York; the author, T. S. Eliot, 34, in London; and the author's representative, lawyer John Quinn, 52, in New York, Eliot's epic poem, *The Waste Land*, is finally published in book form.

Eliot has added extensive academic-style annotations to increase the number of pages to a more traditional book size.

According to the agreement worked out by Quinn, the complete poem appeared in the American literary magazine *The Dial* in November, and Eliot was awarded the magazine's annual prize of $2,000. *The Dial* agreed to buy 350 copies of the hardback book from Boni and Liveright, and the book's cover and advertising tout the Dial Prize.

On the suggestion of *The Dial* editor, Gilbert Seldes, 29, Liveright has numbered the 1,000 copies of the first edition to give them more value and lowered the retail price from $2 to $1.50.

❧❀❧

In London, the author is pleased by the praise he is receiving in print and in letters from friends, for his poem as well as his own literary magazine which he has started, *The Criterion*.

After receiving the first issue, Quinn wrote to him,

 It's a beautiful thing, beautiful printing and on good paper. That first number will be memorable. I hope you can keep it up."

In the midst of all this success, Eliot is still rankled by an anonymous letter he has received. Signed "Your Wellwisher," it contained four three-halfpenny postage stamps.

Eliot knows that this is an insulting reference to his financial situation, and the effort by some of his friends to set up a trust, *Bel Esprit*, to give him extra income so he can leave his day job at Lloyds Bank.

DECEMBER 17, 1922
IRELAND

During the past two weeks:

- The Irish Free State becomes official, and W. T. Cosgrave, 42, becomes its first head of government.

- The Parliament of Northern Ireland votes to remain—to stay in the United Kingdom, opting out of the new Free State. The Irish Boundary Commission is created to determine where to draw the line between the two.

- In Leinster House, the Irish Senate, which includes poet and playwright **William Butler Yeats**, 57, and his doctor, Oliver St. John Gogarty, 44, meets for the first time.

- Messages of congratulations are received from King George V, 57, and Pope Pius XI, 65.

- The first domestic stamps for the new country are issued.

This evening, the last British garrisons leave from Dublin Port to return to the UK.

And the Civil War continues.

British troops leaving and Irish Free State troops arriving

❧ DECEMBER 19, 1922 ❧
HOGARTH HOUSE, RICHMOND; AND
182 EBURY STREET, BELGRAVIA, LONDON

Virginia Woolf, 40, is looking forward to dinner tonight with her new friend, fellow author Vita Sackville-West, 30, at Vita's posh home in Belgravia.

Virginia and her husband **Leonard**, 42, met the Nicholsons—Vita and her husband Sir Harold Nicholson, 36—just a few days ago at a party hosted by **Virginia's** brother-in-law, art critic **Clive Bell**, 41, at his Gordon Square house.

Clive had arranged the get-together specifically so the two couples could meet. **Clive** had passed on to **Virginia** Vita's comment that she feels **Woolf** is the best female writer in England. This

Vita Sackville-West

from an already established British writer is encouraging to **Virginia**, who just published her third novel, *Jacob's Room*, this time with the **Woolfs'** own Hogarth Press.

After their meeting, **Virginia** noted in her diary,

    " The lovely gifted aristocratic Sackville-West…is a grenadier; hard, handsome, manly, inclined to a double chin. She is a pronounced Sapphist and [Vita] may, thinks [English composer] Ethel Sands, have an eye on me, old though I am."

❧❀❧

Meanwhile, a bit less than an hour away on the District Line, Vita has been telling Harold how impressed she is by **Virginia**:

❝ I've rarely taken such a fancy to anyone…I have quite lost my heart… I simply adore **Virginia**…She is both detached and human, silent till she wants to say something and then says it supremely well. She dresses quite atrociously."

❧ CHRISTMAS, 1922 ❧
DEL MONTE RANCH, NEAR TAOS, NEW MEXICO

Happy Christmas!
This has never been the favorite holiday for English writer David Herbert Lawrence, 37. Last year he was fine staying in bed with a persistent case of flu.

But this year Lawrence is actually enjoying himself. His American publisher, Thomas Seltzer, 47, and his wife Adele, 46, have come to visit Lawrence and his German wife Frieda, 43, at their ranch here.

In preparation for the trip, Frieda had written to Adele:

❝ You will find it a different sort of life after New York—bring warm clothes and *old* clothes and riding things if you like riding—It's primitive to say the least of it—but plenty of wood and cream and chickens."

With the clean, dry scent of pine-log fires coming from the fireplace, the two couples have been cooking bread, roasted chicken, Christmas pudding, and mince pie. The Lawrences' patron, who invited him to come live here, Mabel Dodge, 43, has given them a puppy, Bibbles, who has kept the visitors entertained.

Their hosts have taken the Seltzers to see nearby hot springs, pueblos, and Santa Fe.

In the evenings, the publisher and his author talk shop together. One recurring topic is *Ulysses*, the new novel by Irishman James Joyce, 40. Lawrence thinks it's "tiresome," but hasn't really read the whole thing.

Their other topic of conversation is Lawrence's agent, Robert Mountsier, 34. Seltzer is trying to convince Lawrence that he doesn't really need an agent to be published by Thomas Seltzer, Inc. Hasn't he always treated his authors fairly? And Mountsier has made it clear that he didn't even like Lawrence's most recent novels *Aaron's Rod* or *Kangaroo*.

The Lawrences have invited Mountsier to visit too, paying his train fare from New York with David's royalties. Luckily, the terribly anti-Semitic Mountsier won't be arriving until the day before the Seltzers leave.

But he's staying for four weeks. Lawrence isn't looking forward to that.

❧ LATE DECEMBER, 1922 ❧
MONTMARTRE, PARIS; AND WEST END, LONDON

In Paris, the Ballets Russes is performing *Parade*, which they premiered here five years ago with music by Erik Satie, 56, and a scenario written by Jean Cocteau, 33. The scenery, curtains and costumes are all created in a Cubist style by Spanish artist Pablo Picasso, 41, who gets his own ovation when the audience stands up to cheer, facing the box he is seated in.

Jean Cocteau

But the big success of the season is Cocteau's production of *Antigone*, his "contraction" of Sophocles' original, as Cocteau calls it.

Picasso also received a round of cheers during the rehearsals for the play, when Cocteau brought him to an almost bare set, with just some masks and a violet-blue and white backdrop, and told the painter to create a hot, sunny day.

Picasso paced the stage. Picked up a piece of red chalk. Rubbed the white boards with it until they looked like marble. Dipped a brush in a bottle of ink. Drew some lines on the background and blackened in a few spaces.

Three Doric columns appeared. All those watching applauded.

Cocteau also persuaded Coco Chanel, 39, to design the heavy Scotch woolen costumes for Oedipus' daughters.

Antigone is packing them in at the 100-year-old Théâtre de l'Atelier, owned by the actor and drama teacher Charles Dullin, 37, who directed the production and appears in it as well. Dullin's mother pawned the family's furniture and silverware to get enough money for Charles to buy and renovate this theatre.

Cocteau himself is playing the part of the Chorus, and also in the cast is one of Dullin's students, Antonin Artaud, 26. The music for the play has been written by Swiss composer Arthur Honegger, 30, and the lead is played by a Romanian dancer, Génica Athanasiou, 25, who speaks so little French she had to learn her lines syllable by syllable. As a reward for her efforts, Cocteau has dedicated the production to her.

Each evening begins with a short curtain-raiser by Italian playwright Luigi Pirandello, 55, who had success last year with his *Six Characters in Search of an Author.*

The names Picasso, Chanel and Pirandello are what initially drew the crowds. However, now that *Antigone* is a big hit, Cocteau is becoming a cult figure among young men who show up in large groups to applaud each night. Some have even been hanging around outside Cocteau's house and climbing up the lamp post just to get a look at him.

❧⚬✿

In London's West End, German Count Harry Kessler, 54, is enjoying theatre while visiting the city for the first time since the Great War broke out. He confides his impressions to his diary,

    ❝ Not much change in the shops. They are as good class and as elegant as they used to be. But there is no longer the astounding amount of hustle and luxury as in 1914 and which is still to be met in Paris. It can be sensed that the country has become poorer and the shoppers rarer…[At the theatre] to my astonishment, at least half the men in the stalls were in lounge suits, the rest in dinner jackets, and only five or six in tails. A real revolution or, more accurately, the symptom of such."

❧ DECEMBER 27, 1922 ❧
SCRIBNER'S, 153-157 FIFTH AVENUE, NEW YORK CITY, NEW YORK

Max Perkins, 38, has been here at Scribner's for 12 years now. He's mostly worked on his authors' novels, short story collections and non-fiction works. This is the first time he's been asked to edit a play.

Perkins' star novelist, **F. Scott Fitzgerald**, 26, has had his second novel, *The Beautiful and Damned*, followed by his second story collection, *Tales of the Jazz Age*, published this year. Both are doing well.

Scott is working on a third novel, but is currently sidetracked by writing this play, originally titled *Gabriel's Trombone*. He has decided on a new title, *The Vegetable: From President to Postman*.

Perkins agreed to read it and give **Scott** some feedback, which he sent to him yesterday:

> " I've read your play three times and I think more highly of its possibilities on the third reading than ever before;—but I am also more strongly convinced that these possibilities are far from being realized on account of the handling of the story in the second act [in which the main character has drunken fantasies of becoming president]...You seem to lose sense of your true motive...Satirize as much as you can...but keep one eye always on your chief motive. Throughout the entire wild second act there would still be a kind of 'wild logic.'...
>
> My only excuse for all this verbiage is, that so good in conception is your motive, so true your characters, so splendidly imaginative your invention, and so altogether above the mere literate the whole scheme, that no one could help but greatly desire to see it all equal in execution. If it were a comparative trifle, like many a short story, it wouldn't much matter...To save space, I've omitted most of the 'I thinks,' 'It seems to mes,' and 'I may be wrong buts': They would be, however, understood."

❧ END OF DECEMBER, 1922 ❧
NEW YORK CITY, NEW YORK;
LONDON; AND PARIS

Rumors are flying around New York City that a group of con men are planning to print cheap, bootleg copies of the scandalous new novel *Ulysses* by Irishman James Joyce, 40.

These literary pirates plan to take advantage of the fact that 400 copies of the banned book were destroyed when they arrived in this country from the publisher in Paris, American bookstore owner Sylvia Beach, 35. Booksellers here would love to get their hands on some copies, which are going for as much as $100 each on the black market. Some are even being smuggled over the border by an American book lover who commutes to work in Canada.

One of Beach's American friends has written to her, lamenting,

❝ It is too absurd that *Ulysses* cannot circulate over here. I feel a bitter resentment over my inability to read it."

In his law offices, attorney John Quinn, 52, who has helped to fund the publication and promotion of *Ulysses*, knows that getting an injunction against these literary thieves would be too expensive. They'd pass the printing plates on to more thieves in a different state and he'd spend all his time getting injunctions, state after state.

Quinn does have a creative solution, however. If he were to alert his nemesis, John Sumner, 46, the head of the New York Society for the Suppression of Vice (NYSSV), that copies of the book that he himself—and the court—have deemed obscene are circulating, Sumner would put the time and effort into tracking down the gangs and stopping publication before the counterfeit copies hit the streets.

How ironic. Sumner was the guy Quinn fought in court to keep *Ulysses* legal.

The U. S. Customs authorities are trying to confiscate every copy of the novel that enters the country and then store them in the General Post Office Building. The local officials appeal to the Post Office Department in Washington, D. C., for instructions about what to do with the 400 copies of this 700-page book they are storing. The Feds respond that the book is obscene and all copies should be burned.

So they are.

Some copies of *Ulysses* do make it safely into the States, shipped from London where they had been taken apart and wrapped in newspapers. These are from the second edition, published this fall in Paris by the Egoist Press, owned by Joyce's patron, Harriet Shaw Weaver, 46.

When Harriet learned that at least 400 copies had been burned in New York, she simply ordered up 400 more.

Back in March, when the first major review of *Ulysses* appeared in *The Observer*—which considered the novel a work of genius, but concluded,

John Sumner

❝ Yes. This is undoubtedly an obscene book."

—a concerned citizen passed the clipping on to the Home Office, which contacted the undersecretary of state requesting the names and location of any bookstores selling *Ulysses*. Weaver also thinks they sent a detective to follow her as she personally makes deliveries to each shop which has ordered copies to be sold under the counter only to special customers.

The Home Office also became aware of much more negative reviews of *Ulysses*, which led the undersecretary to call it "unreadable, unquotable, and unreviewable." He issued instructions that copies entering the country should be seized, but his order is only provisional, and he doesn't have a copy himself to read. So the Home Office requests an official opinion from the Crown Protection Service (CPS).

In the meantime, a British customs officer, doing his duty, takes a package from a passenger who landed at Croydon Airport in London, and, recognizing it as the banned *Ulysses*, flips to page 704 to see why. He confiscates the book on orders from His Majesty's Customs and Excise Office, but the passenger complains that it is a work of art, praised by many reviewers, and on sale in bookshops in London as well as Paris.

Customs and Excise seizes the book but sends it on to the Home Office for a ruling.

This copy of *Ulysses* makes its way through the bureaucracy and finally lands on the desk of Sir Archibald Bodkin, 60, Director of Public Prosecutions at the CPS and scourge of the suffragettes whom his officers had routinely arrested and abused.

Bodkin only had to read the final chapter to issue his decision. Which he did two days before the end of 1922:

“ “ I have not had the time nor, I may add, the inclination to read through this book. I have, however, read pages 690 to 732. I am entirely unable to appreciate how those pages are relevant to the rest of the book, or, indeed, what the book itself is about. I can discover no story, there is no introduction which might give a key to its purpose, and the pages above mentioned, written as they are as if composed by a more or less illiterate vulgar woman, form an entirely detached part of this production. In my opinion, there is…a great deal more than mere vulgarity or coarseness, there is a great deal of unmitigated filth and obscenity…[Customs should confiscate and burn all copies, and if there is public protest] the answer will be that it is filthy and filthy books are not allowed to be imported into this country."

End of.

❧❀❧

In Paris, at the bookstore where it all began, Sylvia Beach is selling increasing numbers of *Ulysses* every day. Customers who come in asking for it leave with copies of all Joyce's books.

By the end of the year, James Joyce is her best seller, beating out William Blake, Herman Melville, and, one of Sylvia's favorites, Walt Whitman.

Sylvia Beach and James Joyce

My Irishman, Tony Dixon, and me

🎔 DECEMBER 31, 1922/ 🎔 JANUARY 1, 1923
IRELAND, ENGLAND, FRANCE AND AMERICA

At the end of the third year of the 1920s...

In Ireland, despite living in the middle of a Civil War, and the death of his 82-year-old father this past February, poet and playwright **William Butler Yeats**, 57, has had a pretty good year.

He is enjoying his appointment to the newly formed Senate of the Irish Free State, engineered by his friend and family doctor, Oliver St. John Gogarty, 44, who managed to get himself appointed as well.

Much to **Yeats'** surprise, the position comes with an income, making it the first paying job he has ever had. The money, as he writes to a friend,

> 66 of which I knew nothing when I accepted, will compensate me somewhat for the chance of being burned or bombed. We are a fairly distinguished body, much more so than the lower house, and should get much government into our hands…How long our war is to last nobody knows. Some expect it to end this Xmas and some equally well informed expect another three years."

Indeed, although **Senator Yeats** has been provided with an armed guard at his house, two bullets were shot through the front door of his family home in Merrion Square on Christmas Eve.

A few blocks away the Abbey Theatre, which he helped to found 18 years ago, is still doing well. *John Bull's Other Island*, a play by his fellow Dubliner, George Bernard Shaw, 66, is being performed, starring part-time actor and full-time civil servant Barry Fitzgerald, 34.

Yeats has been awarded an Honorary D. Litt. From Trinity College, Dublin. He writes to a friend that this makes him feel "that I have become a personage."

※ ※ ※

In England, at Monk's House, their country home in East Sussex, the **Woolfs**, **Virginia**, 40, and **Leonard**, 42, are reviewing the state of their five-year-old publishing company, the Hogarth Press.

They have added 37 members to the Press' subscriber list and have agreed to publish a new poem by their friend, American ex-pat Thomas Stearns Eliot, 34, called *The Waste Land* early in the new year. **Virginia** has donated £50 to a fund to help "poor Tom," as she calls him, who still has a full-time day job at Lloyds Bank. Eliot takes the £50, as well as the $2,000 *Dial* magazine prize he has been awarded in America and sets up a trust fund for himself and his wife Vivien, 34.

The road outside Monk's House

The Hogarth Press has published six titles this year, the same as last. But most important to **Virginia**, one of them, *Jacob's Room*, is her first novel *not* published by her hated stepbrother, Gerald Duckworth, 52. She can write as she pleases now.

Most interesting to **Virginia** at the end of this year is her newfound friendship with another successful English novelist, Vita Sackville-West, 30. The **Woolfs** have been spending lots of time with Vita and her husband, Sir Harold Nicolson, 36.

Virginia writes in her diary,

66   The human soul, it seems to me, orients itself afresh every now and then. It is doing so now…No one can see it whole, therefore. The best of us catch a glimpse of a nose, a shoulder, something turning away, always in movement."

❋❋❋

In France, American ex-pats **Gertrude Stein**, 48, and her partner, **Alice B. Toklas**, 45, are vacationing in St. Remy. They came for a month and have decided to stay for the duration of the winter.

Stein is pleased that her *Geography and Plays* has recently been published by Four Seas back in Boston. This eclectic collection of stories, poems, plays and language experiments that she has written over the past decade comes with an encouraging introduction by one of her American friends, established novelist **Sherwood Anderson**, 46. He says that **Gertrude's** work is among the most important being written today, and lives "among the little housekeeping words, the swaggering bullying street-corner words, the honest working, money-saving words."

The volume also contains her 1913 poem, "Sacred Emily," which includes a phrase **Stein** repeats often, "Rose is a rose is a rose is a rose." **Alice** is thinking of using that as part of the logo for **Gertrude's** personal stationery.

Stein and **Toklas** are hopeful that *Geography and Plays* will help her blossoming reputation as a serious writer. For now, they are going to send some fruit to one of their new American friends back in Paris, foreign correspondent for the *Toronto Star*, **Ernest Hemingway**, 23, and his lovely wife Hadley, 31.

In America, free-lance writer **Dorothy Parker**, 29, has had a terrible year.

She did get her first short story published, "Such a Pretty Little Picture" in this month's issue of *Smart Set*. After years of writing only the light verse that sells easily to New York's magazines and newspapers, **Parker** is starting to branch out and stretch herself more.

However, her stockbroker husband of five years, Edwin Pond Parker II, also 29, finally packed up and moved back to his family in Connecticut.

Parker took up with a would-be playwright from Chicago, Charles MacArthur, 27, who started hanging around with her lunch friends from the Algonquin Hotel. He broke **Dottie's** heart—and her spirit after he contributed only $30 to her abortion. And made himself scarce afterwards.

On Christmas day there were no fewer than eight new plays for **Parker** to review. She had to bundle up against the cold and spend the holiday racing around to see as much of each one as she could. And then go home to no one but her bird Onan ["because he spills his seed"] and her dog Woodrow Wilson.

As she gets ready to jump into 1923, **Parker** works on the type of short poem she has become known for:

"One Perfect Rose"

By **Dorothy Parker**

A single flow'r he sent me, since we met.
All tenderly his messenger he chose;
Deep-hearted, pure, with scented dew still wet—
One perfect rose.
I knew the language of the floweret;
"My fragile leaves," it said, "his heart enclose."
Love long has taken for his amulet
One perfect rose.
Why is it no one ever sent me yet
One perfect limousine, do you suppose?
Ah no, it's always just my luck to get
One perfect rose.

You can hear Dorothy Parker read her poem, "One Perfect Rose," here:
https://www.youtube.com/watch?v=iMnv1XNpuwM

TO READ…

Quentin Bell. *Virginia Stephen, 1882-1912*, and *Mrs. Woolf, 1912-1941*. Volumes I and II of his *Virginia Woolf: A Biography*. London: Hogarth Press, 1972. His uncle Leonard Woolf asked him to write it and he did a great job.

A. Scott Berg. *Max Perkins: Editor of Genius*. New York: E. P. Dutton, 1978. The full excellent biography, by the Pulitzer-prize winning *Lindbergh* and Katharine Hepburn biographer.

Kevin Birmingham. *The Most Dangerous Book: The Battle for James Joyce's* Ulysses. New York: The Penguin Press, 2014. Detailed look at the struggle to get *Ulysses* published. God bless Sylvia Beach.

Michael Cunningham. *The Hours*. New York: Farrar, Straus and Giroux, 1998. A well-deserved Pulitzer went to this creative and fascinating novel that, like *Mrs. Dalloway*, weaves three stories in different time periods together. Woolf's original title for her novel was *The Hours*.

Kathleen Dixon Donnelly. *Manager as Muse: Max Perkins' Work with F. Scott Fitzgerald, Ernest Hemingway, and Thomas Wolfe*. Birmingham, UK: K. Donnelly Communications, 2014. 'Nuff said.

Kathleen Dixon Donnelly. *"Such Friends": The Literary 1920s*. Pittsburgh, PA: K. Donnelly Communications, 2021. A collection of my blogs about what was happening 100 years ago. Volumes I and II, covering 1920 and 1921, are available on Amazon in print and e-book formats.

Noel Riley Fitch. *Sylvia Beach and the Lost Generation: A History of Literary Paris in the Twenties and Thirties*. New York: W. W. Norton and Co. A detailed and fascinating look at this amazing woman and her friendships with the other characters in Paris at the time.

Kevin Fitzpatrick. *The Dorothy Parker Society*. His excellent website [https://dorothyparker.com/book-shop] includes books by and about Parker and the Round Table. All of his are good, along with the Facebook group and his walking tours in Manhattan. Highly recommended.

Brendan Gill. *Here at* The New Yorker. New York: Random House, 1975. The semi-official biography of the magazine up until the 70s.

Bill Goldstein. *The World Broke in Two: Virginia Woolf, T. S. Eliot, D. H. Lawrence, E. M. Forster and the Year that Changed Literature.* New York: Henry Holt and Company, 2017. Centered mostly in London, he does a good job of connecting these four separate lives.

Arlen J. Hansen. *Expatriate Paris: A Cultural and Literary Guide to Paris of the 1920s.* New York: Arcade Publishing, 2012. In an almanac format organized by areas of the city, this chronicles who was there and where they lived. Good to take with you when you go.

Joseph M. Hassett. *The* Ulysses *Trials: Beauty and Truth Meet the Law.* Dublin: Lilliput Press, 2016. He brings a lawyer's point of view to both trials. And he really doesn't like John Quinn.

Ernest Hemingway. *A Moveable Feast.* New York: Charles Scribner's Sons, 1964. His version of events, as he remembered them years later.

Kevin Jackson. *Constellation of Genius: 1922: Modernism Year One.* London: Hutchinson, 2012. A month by month listing of what was happening in this important year for literature. Good as a reference but no pictures!

Brenda Maddox. *George's Ghosts: A New Life of W. B. Yeats.* London: Picador, 1999. Focuses on his late-life marriage and is a really good read.

Marion Meade. *Bobbed Hair and Bathtub Gin: Writers Running Wild in the Twenties, Edna St. Vincent Millay, Dorothy Parker, Zelda Fitzgerald, and Edna Ferber.* New York: Harcourt, Inc., 2004. Meade does well expanding her Parker research to include the other fabulous women.

Marion Meade. *Dorothy Parker: What Fresh Hell Is This?* London: Heinemann, 1988. The best. Excellent biography and the basis for the film, *Mrs. Parker and the Vicious Circle* as well as the A&E *Biography* program.

James R. Mellow. *Charmed Circle: Gertrude Stein and Company.* New York: Avon Books, 1974. The best overall book about this era and the characters in Paris.

Emily Midorikawa and Emma Claire Sweeney. *A Secret Sisterhood.* London: Aurum Press, 2017. A terrific look at the literary friendships of Austen, Bronte, Eliot and Woolf by two great friends of mine in the UK.

Ulick O'Connor. *Celtic Dawn: A Portrait of the Irish Literary Renaissance.* London: Black Swan, 1984. The best history of the whole time period and the characters involved.

B. L. Reid. *The Man from New York: John Quinn and His Friends.* New York: Oxford University Press, 1968. Read it if you must, but it's a slog and it makes this absolutely fascinating man seem boring.

Michael Reynolds. *Hemingway: The Paris Years.* Cambridge, MA: Basil Blackwell, 1989. Just one part of the best multi-volume biography and also one of the most detailed accounts of Paris at the time.

Diane Souhami. *Gertrude and Alice.* New York: Pandora, 1991. Better than a biography of either one of them, the author writes about both equally and, most interesting, about their relationship.

Frances Spalding. *Vanessa Bell.* London: Weidenfield and Nicolson, 1983. In writing about Roger Fry she discovered Vanessa Bell and wrote this definitive biography. I'm including this one of her books, because it's my favorite. But anything by her is great.

Gertrude Stein. *The Autobiography of Alice B. Toklas.* New York: Vintage Books, 1990. If you've ever been afraid to read Stein, this is the place to start. Definitely her point of view, and a wonderful romp.

Colm Toibin. *Lady Gregory's Toothbrush.* London: Picador, 2003. The title comes from her comment after the *Playboy* riots, "It's the old battle between those who use a toothbrush and those who don't." By the Irish author of the novel *Brooklyn*.

Colm Toibin. *Mad, Bad, Dangerous to Know: The Fathers of Wilde, Yeats and Joyce.* London: Penguin, 2018. Terrific book about three amazing Irishmen—and their sons.

W. B. Yeats. *Selected Poetry.* Ed. with an introduction and notes by A. Norman Jeffares. London: Macmillan, 1990. The best collection of his best poems; the introduction is a good overall mini-biography.

TO WATCH...

Albert Nobbs. [2011] Glenn Close, Janet McTeer. There aren't really any feature films about the Irish Literary Renaissance—and neither is this one. But it is a beautiful evocation of Dublin in the late 19th century. A long time labor of love for Close, it netted her and McTeer Oscar nominations.

Carrington. [1995] Jonathan Pryce, Emma Thompson. Excellent film about the relationship between Lytton Strachey and his partner, Dora Carrington. The beginning scenes show the Bloomsbury group at Vanessa Bell's Sussex house, Charleston, where it was filmed.

Genius. [2016] Colin Firth, Jude Law, Laura Linney. Max Perkins editing a novel doesn't sound like much of a basis for a film, but Firth's Perkins and Law's bombastic Tom Wolfe strike just the right note. Linney as Perkins' wife is the only American actor as a main character, and all filming was done in the UK. Go figure.

The Hours. [2002] Nicole Kidman, Julianne Moore, Meryl Streep. Award-winning film version of Michael Cunningham's book (see above). The scenes of Los Angeles in the 1950s were all filmed where we lived in Hollywood, Florida.

Midnight in Paris. [2011] Owen Wilson, Kathy Bates. Directed by Woody Allen, who is in love with the city and the time period. "I am Dali!"

Mrs. Dalloway. [1997] Vanessa Redgrave, Natascha McElhone. Directed by Marleen Gorris, Redgrave was a great choice to portray Virginia's favorite heroine.

Mrs. Parker and the Vicious Circle. [1994] Jennifer Jason Leigh, Scott Campbell, Matthew Broderick. Excellent film based on Meade's biography of Parker (see above). It has the look and feel of the time and the characters.

Yes, she did mumble like that, so you might want to have the rewind button handy. There are numerous clips on YouTube.

Paris Was a Woman. [1996] This terrific documentary focuses on the female relationships in Paris in the 1920s, with a lot about Sylvia Beach's support of James Joyce.

The Ten-Year Lunch. [1987] Good documentary about the whole Algonquin group, narrated by Heywood Broun's son, CBS sportscaster Heywood Hale Broun. Includes interviews with Marc Connelly, Helen Hayes, Ruth Gordon and Averell Harriman, among others. A bit outdated, but they're all dead anyway.

TO VISIT...

The Abbey Theatre. [https://www.abbeytheatre.ie/]. On Abbey Street in Dublin, the theatre came up with a creative schedule for a COVID 2020 season, so there is a lot you can experience on line at their site and on Facebook. They also have a detailed archive of all their productions.

The Algonquin Hotel. [https://www.algonquinhotel.com/]. At 59 West 44th Street, the hotel has been refurbished many times and each new owner has pledged to retain its literary history. The latest Algonquin cat, Hamlet, has his own Facebook page.

BloggingWoolf. [https://bloggingwoolf.wordpress.com/]. Run by Paula Maggio of Kent State University, this is one of the best blogs to follow for all things Woolfian.

Cambridge Ladies' Dining Society 1890-1914. [https://akennedysmith. com/]. Dr. Ann Kennedy Smith's specialty subject is women who came to Cambridge, England, in the 1870s and 1880s, and she does a great job of making them come to life.

Charleston Farmhouse. [https://www.charleston.org.uk/]. On your next European trip—Go. You'll have to drive or take a taxi from nearby Lewes, but it is well worth it, particularly during their May festival.

Coole Park. [https://www.coolepark.ie/]. Lady Gregory's home about 35km south of Galway City, near Gort, is now a national park, without the house but with the autograph tree. Well worth a visit next time you are driving around the west of Ireland.

The Dorothy Parker Society. [https://www.facebook.com/groups/ dorothyparkersociety]. This Facebook group is run by Kevin Fitzpatrick and you can find all of his terrific books there. When you're planning to go to New York again, check out his walking tours. For 20 years he has been keeping the flame with events and publications. Highly recommended.

The Dublin Literary Pub Crawl. [https://www.dublinpubcrawl.com/]. My main Dublin tip, particularly for your first night there. Two actors lead a group of tourists around the main part of the city, stopping to do scenes from Irish literature and theatre, punctuated by drinks in pubs. Great way to get the lay of the land. Until it's safe to travel again, you can buy their book from the site.

Monk's House. [https://www.nationaltrust.org.uk/monks-house]. Virginia and Leonard's country home is part of the National Trust, well worth a visit, and not far from Charleston.

The National Library of Ireland. [www.nli.ie]. The Library has the best exhibit about Yeats and all his "such friends," and I've seen a lot of them. You can access it online and, eventually, in person. Great gift shop—and, ladies, use the downstairs restroom. Trust me.

Philomena Mason. [philomenamason.wordpress.com]. is an Irish playwright and a friend of mine. She has written plays on Lady Gregory and her husband, Sir William, as well as other Irish characters from history, which have been performed in Ireland and the UK. They are delightful. Excerpts are up on her new website, and she will be adding info in the future.

Shakespeare and Company. [https://www.facebook.com/groups/131979076789]. Until it's safe to travel again, you can join their Facebook group. The real shop is on a totally different site, directly across from Notre Dame, but worth a visit. Then go sit in one of the cafes. They are still there.

Sissinghurst. [https://www.nationaltrust.org.uk/sissinghurst-castle-garden]. Vita Sackville-West's home is known especially for its gorgeous gardens. If you can, stay at the B&B on the grounds.

Something Rhymed. [https://somethingrhymed.com/]. The basis for Emily Midorikawa and Emma Claire Sweeney's book, *The Secret Sisterhood* (see above), their blog postings are all about female literary friendships. Like Mabel Dodge and Gertrude Stein (and Alice B. Toklas), for example. Or search for Dorothy Parker and Elinor Wylie.

"Such Friends." [Suchfriends.wordpress.com]. On the blog I am currently chronicling The Literary 1920s. Hopefully, there will be seven more books.

"Such Friends": Virginia Woolf and the Bloomsbury Group. [www.voicemap.me]. My own walking tour of the area is available to download for your mobile or computer.

Thoor Ballylee. [https://yeatsthoorballylee.org/home/]. Yeats' tower, "with the river on the first floor," as Ezra Pound said, is near Coole Park, and also worth the trip when it is open again. They often sponsor events in the summer around his June birthday.

ABOUT THE AUTHOR

Kathleen Dixon Donnelly, Ph.D.

Kathleen Dixon Donnelly has been involved in teaching and the creative process for more than 40 years. Her thesis for her MBA from Duquesne University in her hometown of Pittsburgh, Pennsylvania, was *Manager as Muse, Maxwell Perkins' Work with F. Scott Fitzgerald, Ernest Hemingway and Thomas Wolfe*, available on Amazon in both print and e-book versions.

"Such Friends": The Literary 1920s is based in part on her dissertation for her Ph.D. in Communications from Dublin City University, on the creative development of writers in early 20th century salons.

She has led walking and driving tours of Dublin and Coole Park in Ireland; London and Sussex in England; and the Left Bank of Paris. You can walk with her through Bloomsbury by downloading her tour, *"Such Friends": Virginia Woolf and the Bloomsbury Group* from the site www.voicemap.me. She has given numerous presentations about the writers throughout the United Kingdom and the United States at the Southbank Centre, the University of the Third Age, the English Speaking Union, and Osher Lifelong Learning programs.

Kathleen has self-published a series of books from her blogs as *Gypsy Teacher*, chronicling her voyages on Semester at Sea and relocation to the United Kingdom, available on Amazon.

She retired as a senior lecturer in both the School of Media and Business School at Birmingham [UK] City University to return to her hometown of Pittsburgh, Pennsylvania, where she lives with her Irish-American husband Tony Dixon and their two cats, Gertrude Stein and Robert Benchley.

You can contact her by email at kaydee@gypsyteacher.com, through Twitter @SuchFriends, or through her blog, www.suchfriends.wordpress.com.

Made in the USA
Middletown, DE
30 October 2022

13779685R00165